So Close, I Can Feel
God's Breath

So Close, I Can Feel
God's Breath

Dr. Beverly Rose

SALTRIVER®

An Imprint of
Tyndale House Publishers, Inc.

Visit Tyndale's exciting Web site at www.tyndale.com

TYNDALE is a registered trademark of Tyndale House Publishers, Inc.

SaltRiver and the SaltRiver logo are registered trademarks of Tyndale House Publishers, Inc.

So Close, I Can Feel God's Breath

Designed by Joseph Sapulich

Library of Congress Cataloging-in-Publication Data
Rose, Beverly.
    So close, I can feel God's breath : experiencing His nearness in thin places / Beverly Rose.
       p. cm.
ISBN-13: 978-1-4143-0724-4 (sc)
ISBN-10: 1-4143-0724-1 (sc)
1. Spiritual life—Christianity. I. Title.
BV4501.3.R67 2006
248.4—dc22   2005029583

Printed in the United States of America

12 11 10 09 08 07 06
 7   6   5   4   3   2   1

"To know this Presence is the most desirable state imaginable for anyone. To live surrounded by this sense of God is not only beautiful and desirable, but it is imperative!"

A. W. Tozer

This book is dedicated to
my father—
who, in love,
dared to brave the
thinnest of places.

CONTENTS

Preface

Imagine a place between seashore and sea, earth and sky, here and now and heaven to come—a place where the veil between this life and the next is so thin you can almost touch the very hand of God. That mysterious place on the ethereal edge of existence has been known for centuries as a "thin place." You can see it for yourself today—if you know where to look for the unseen.

God waits for us in thin places, beckoning us to grasp the beauty of his handiwork—and reach out for the hand that made it. He breathes in our lives and hearts in miraculous ways, his mysterious stirrings as ubiquitous as radio waves invisibly reverberating within earshot—and often just as silent. Yet if we orient our internal antennae to the Divine, we may just discover what our eyes *can* see and our ears *can* hear.

I long to be in the thick of things with God in thin

places, those spiritual sweet spots of life that are here, there, and everywhere. I wish to brave the frontier at the very edge of existence to assure myself again and again that there is more to life than just existing.

Finding thin places? Fat chance, you may say. That's what I said too, until I found myself beholding a divine spark in my dead mother's eyes as she suddenly returned to life. In that mystifying place between life and death, heaven and earth, I witnessed more than there is—because we are more than what we seem to be.

I awaken every morning in search of God in thin places—God willing, that is. For I am trapped in an unforgiving body afflicted with a neuromuscular disease and rise only by the power of his grace. I know, because several years ago, bedridden and bereft, I met Jesus in the thinnest of all places and was lifted far above circumstance. That is where I try to stay.

Since that remarkable day, I have had many amazing moments when I have felt not only spiritually whole but also physically healed—for the moment. That's because I'm healed in moments—although I've yet to be cured. Nevertheless, such amazing encounters with the Lord give me the promise of an extraordinary life to come and hope in the midst of a life that is far from ordinary.

We don't have to be on thin ice to find ourselves in thin places. They are all around us, even within us. We need only have the determination to uncover what we are destined to discover.

So come along. We are about to embark on a journey to miraculous places. Come sense the lus-

I met Jesus in the thinnest of all places and was lifted far above circumstance. That is where I try to stay.

cious, mystical divinity of a place that lies just beyond your grasp but not your reach. Find the extraordinary in what appears to be the ordinary, seeing for yourself a vision not only of what life is but also of how it can be. Feel the Lord breathe into your heart and soul. Discover the love and grace of God in your everyday relationships. The possibilities are endless, because these amazing places not only evoke our emotions but also enable us to transcend them. You may even discover that you can be transformed, becoming a thin place for others.

Come dare to wonder, for there are wonders all around us and even within us. We may go through life absorbed in the mundane, or we may suddenly find that right in front of our very eyes is a miraculous place. We can spend our days on earth in quiet desperation, waiting for the day we reach heaven, or we can reach for heaven now, catching a glimpse of the unbroken continuum between this life and the next. The miraculous places we experience today are deposits of hope, promises of the glory to come.

Embark on this marvelous spiritual journey, and you may find yourself home, seeing more clearly where you've been and where you're going.

The miraculous places we experience today are deposits of hope, promises of the glory to come.

You need not take my word for it. Nor do you have to believe in thin places. You need only have faith with which to see.

PART 1

What on Earth Is a Thin Place?

Chapter 1

Life on the Edge

Thin places are not only extraordinary places. They are also ordinarily found just this side of the other side.

I long to live life on the edge, braving new frontiers to the very end—as long as on the other side there is a beginning. That's where our story begins: on just an ordinary day in April—at the very end of it all, just this side of the other side.

As a vibrant Florida sun reached its apex in the deep blue sky, I bent over my mother's lifeless body. "Is she dead?" I whispered to myself. I probably should have asked her, but I didn't want to worry her—just in case she really was.

I touched her shoulder. She didn't move. "Oh, dear God, she is dead!" I screamed loudly enough to wake the dead. But not her. "Mom, please don't be dead!" I begged, as if she could control such things. She didn't comment, dramatically increasing the possibility that she was. When it comes to Jewish mothers, death is usually the only explanation for silence.

I placed my hand over her mouth to feel for breath and thought I detected a wisp of air. Or was it just the breeze rattling the shades protecting her from the scorching Florida sun? If only she could have been shielded as easily from the vicissitudes of life.

Frantically, I checked for a pulse. My heart pounded. Hers didn't. Her body grew rigid; her gaze became fixed and glassy. I stared into the faded blue-gray eyes that had once overflowed with love, filled with compassion, sparkled when she laughed, grown intense when she spouted pearls of Yiddish wisdom. I had so often chosen to see life through my mother's eyes because they were so full of life. Now all I could see in them was death. My body froze while my mind raced.

Only minutes before, my mother had awakened me from sound sleep. "I don't feel well." That was all she'd said. I helped her back to her bedroom before she collapsed onto the bed, took several labored breaths, and fell silent.

"Breathe, Mom, breathe!" I shouted over and over again. But she wasn't deaf, just dead. Finally, in resignation, I whispered, "I love you, Mom. I love you." I thought they would be my last words to her.

Then I had an insight. I placed my mouth over hers and blew a stream of air into her lungs. Suddenly she stirred to life. It wasn't long before she took advantage of her newfound breath to speak. "I was floating. It was so nice and peaceful. Then I heard you say 'I love you,' and I decided to come back." *From the dead, Mom?* I wondered. But I dared not ask.

The paramedics finally arrived to rush her to the

emergency room. She was long settled in her hospital bed when I found myself sitting on a bench on the local boardwalk, trying to calm myself down. The death scene may have been over, but the dreadful reruns played on in my mind.

I removed my shoes and headed for the shoreline, laboring hard in the soft sand to make it to the water. It was the same route I had taken so many times before. But this time was different—I could hardly walk. The symptoms that would later be diagnosed as an incurable neuromuscular disease had overtaken my thirtysomething body, leaving me practically bedridden, unemployed, and living with my parents.

Whether or not I could walk, I needed to flee to a place of refuge—to a familiar place of transcendence, where I could be lifted up when the trials of life were getting me down. For years I had made tracks in the moist, packed sand along the edge of that beach, feeling the grains settle comfortably between my toes. It was always a marvel to me how sand, so thoroughly infused by the rising sea, had not yet been claimed by it. Borders are like that. They impart a unique strength and hope, somehow managing to hold a tension between here and there while retaining a distinct place between places for themselves.

One minute she was here and the next, where? My mother's body lay whole on the bed, minus my mother. It was as if she had planned a dinner party, furnishings freshly polished, dinner on the table, then slipped out the back door, leaving a cadre of expectant guests waiting. A hospitable hostess such as my mother could never abide such a lack of courtesy. Besides, the fallout from some of our less than gracious relatives would kill any nice Jewish mother—that is, if she weren't already dead. My mother would have even come back from the dead just to make a socially acceptable exit and save face.

I had to face it. One minute her eyes were vibrant; the next, vacant. One moment they were valuable agents of sight; the next, obsolete orbs. In those eyes I saw her leave and then return as if she had never left. Somewhere in between, I caught a fleeting glimpse of the person who was my mother. She was not the body she was in—and out of—and in again. She was far more.

I was not much of a believer in the afterlife, having been raised in the Jewish religion, which doesn't take an official stance on such matters. Some Jews choose to believe in heaven; others don't. My statement of faith was best expressed by a postcard I had taped to my wall after a particularly enjoyable trip to California many years before. Underneath a drawing of the Golden Gate Bridge was the caption, "There may not be a heaven, but at least there is a San Francisco."

Borders impart a unique strength and hope, somehow managing to hold a tension between here and there while retaining a distinct place between places for themselves.

Even I doubted that in the split second between life and death my mother had gone to "the City by the Bay." *But where did she go?* I wondered—and how had she managed to come back? I knew it was biologically possible to revive a dead person. But for a dead person to travel somewhere and then return because she had heard me say "I love you"? I thought my words had fallen on deaf ears.

Mysteriously, I had experienced a body without a person, while my mother claimed to have been a person without a body. It was as if a flame could exist without a wick. Didn't something have to enable the flame to burn? Was it possible that what I had witnessed in her eyes as she returned to life was a divine spark? I didn't know, but I had come close enough to know that something was there—and only the thinnest veil had kept it from my literal sight. Years later, I would come to realize that in that miraculous, mystifying moment between life and death, I had ventured into a place unlike any other place. That's because thin places are not only extraordinary places. They are also ordinarily found just this side of the other side.

Chapter 2

Discovering the Unseen

Thin places are not only real. They are also part of our everyday reality.

What I experienced the day my mother died and miraculously came back to life was a terrible shock, but the mystery I saw in her eyes wasn't. I had witnessed such mystifying moments in the eyes of my Jewish mother many times before—although thankfully more in the context of life than death.

The Hebrew word for life is *l'chaim*. Said with as much gusto and gurgle as one can muster, it is meant to signify not only life but also celebration of life—even in the midst of sorrow. My mother knew that well, for she frequently straddled the thin border between joy and sadness, hope and despair, while holding on for dear life. I spent many childhood hours perplexed as I stared into her tear-filled eyes that inexplicably brimmed with a light that tears could not extinguish. Was that the light of God? I wondered.

Week after week I would stand in the shadows as my mother lit the Sabbath candles, and week after week I

stood awestruck by the thin place that materialized
before my very eyes. Flickering flames flung themselves
high into the air, as my mother, undaunted, circled her
hands just inches above the burning candles. Then she
would place her fingers over her eyes and begin to pray.
Is that so she can see beyond? I wondered.

Soon she would begin to sob softly, her body shudder-
ing while shadows danced on the wall behind her. It was
an eerie interplay of body and spirit moving in timeless
rhythm. Just moments before, our lives had been filled
with sound and fury. Now we stood motionless in profound silence, witnessing a divine encounter, the depth of
which we could scarcely know or understand.

A tear would invariably find its way down my
mother's hand and splash onto the white linen of the
tablecloth—a reminder of an earlier time and place when,
as a child, she sat at the Sabbath table, her eyes filling
with tears, as she and her poor, starving family salivated
over the prized meal, which had cost the bulk of her
father's earnings for the week. Dressed in the best of her
tattered clothes, she would watch her ailing mother light
candles atop precious brass candlesticks, prized possessions that had been hurriedly snatched as her parents fled
Russia to escape deadly pogroms (raids against Jews).

My mother's childhood tears were as much of joy in
receiving the precious Sabbath bounty once a week as
they were of sorrow that she had to starve so many other
days. Yet, over the years, her tears became more reminis-
cent of past sorrows than of joys.

As I watched her aging body shudder as her sobbing
grew louder, I wondered, What was she saying to God—
and was he answering? I could not know. But when my
anguished mother removed her tearstained hands from

her face, she often revealed an angelic expression. There was a profound peace in her eyes, a peace clearly not from this life but from a place between this world and the next—a place I longed to be. I would peer deeply into her eyes, hoping for a glimpse of what she had witnessed, but I could not see beyond. That's when my fascination with thin places first began—as I struggled to grasp what lay just beyond my reach.

The Baal Shem, a Jewish sage, once stated, "Replete is the world with a spiritual radiance, replete with sublime and marvelous secrets."[1] I gained glimpses of those marvelous secrets in that timeless Sabbath candle-lighting ritual that would come and go like clockwork, leaving behind lingering images shrouded in mystery from some other place in the midst of this one. Those moments left me groping for enlightenment well into the week until the next lighting of the Sabbath candles revived unanswerable questions once again.

Years later, I would come to realize that I wasn't the first to experience such amazing thinness. The early Celtic Christians believed in places of thinness centuries before I stumbled upon such things. They called them thin places, which they believed were holy, Spirit-filled geographical sites lying on the border between earth and heaven. They even founded monasteries on assumed sacred spots to increase the likelihood of spiritual communion with the other world.

In their journeys, the early Celts were forever marking places along the way as sacred. The landscapes they crossed are still littered with monuments and ruins that have become stopping places where people can pause and reflect, and perhaps even be transformed. One of those sites is Croagh Patrick, the holy mountain in County

Mayo, Ireland. This majestic mountain is named after Ireland's patron saint, who is said to have climbed to the peak—one of the highest in Ireland—and from that lofty vantage point blessed the people. Today it remains a powerful and mysterious place, inspiring author Michael Mullen to write: "On this arid summit, where the winds blow hard, where no root takes hold, where distance seems infinite and heaven close, the spirit is tested and replenished . . . for the pilgrim has reached a thin place, where one steps into the highest dimension of one's existence."[2]

The Celts not only found thinness in sacred sites but also in the sheer beauty of nature, which they believed manifested God's handiwork and contained his Spirit. As a child, I found that divine Spirit in natural beauty all around me. I often spent hours comfortably seated high above the world in a maple tree in our backyard, snuggled in a notch where two branches joined. Perched high in that tree, I not only achieved oneness with nature but also communion with God in a still higher place. It was there, lifted above this world, on the border with the next, that I truly found blessed kinship and belonging.

Each time I climbed to my lofty vantage point, I couldn't wait to take in the wonders that surrounded me. Inhaling deep breaths, I savored the lushness of life in the sweet smell of bark and greenery. Opening my eyes wide, I welcomed the budding fruit trees that labored to birth their abundant bounties. Turning my cheek to the wind, I closed my eyes and delighted in the soft breezes that brushed my cheek. I could almost hear

Lifted above this world, on the border with the next, I found blessed kinship and belonging.

God breathing his name. Did you ever notice that saying the name of God sounds almost like breathing? Try saying *Yahweh.* As Rabbi Kushner observes, "The Y's and the H's don't interrupt the flow of sound the way most consonants would."[3] It is more like breathing than speaking.

That was how I communicated with God as a child: not through words but breath to Breath, spirit to Spirit. Such experiences led me to daydream for hours about a mystical realm that lay just beyond the world I could see. *Is it really possible to journey over the rainbow,* I wondered, *the world at my back, heaven ahead, and in between a magical place colored with every color of—well, the rainbow? Even more intriguing, if such miraculous places actually exist, who is there?*

Turning my cheek to the wind, I closed my eyes and delighted in the soft breezes that brushed my cheek. I could almost hear God breathing his name.

Some might assume that my thoughts were just the product of an overactive imagination. I believe they were intuitions of a marvelous reality. Children can experience things of the Spirit in a way few adults can. Their souls can sing for joy without embarrassment, while adults sing self-consciously, wondering if their voices are good enough. Their spirits can laugh for the sheer fun of laughing, while adults usually laugh only when they find something funny.

As a child, I delighted in thin places everywhere. That's not unusual. Modern-day scholars believe that thin places can be found anywhere the love and grace of God touches us—anyplace human and Divine meet in amazing intimacy. Mahatma Gandhi once observed, "There is an indefinable mysterious Power that pervades everything. I feel it, though I do not see it. It is this unseen Power which makes itself felt and yet defies all proof."[4] Gandhi believed this mysterious power to be God. Only later would I understand the source of that power to be Jesus Christ, and access to that power a personal relationship with him—which makes a Christian's experience of thin places different from all others. Later I would not only come to know the fullness of that power but also discover that even in unforgiving places the grace of Jesus can be found, giving us hope of transcendence beyond the sometimes cruel and seemingly random events of life—hope that we are part of something far more significant than our own fragile, limited lives.

Ironically, it was my Jewish mother who prepared the way for me to embrace Jesus in a very thin place. For she imparted to me a capacity to believe that there is more to life than what we see—and it is the unseen, more real than reality itself, that gets us through. She learned this from our ancestors, especially the early Hebrews, who had experienced struggle and redemption in astonishing places of thinness. In fact, God was so present at that time that, as Kushner observes, "For the biblical mind, the existence of God was too obvious to require a statement of faith."[5] In the ancient world, God's Spirit, Ruach, was in the very wind.

In my mother's world, God had been just as present more times than she could count—or I could witness. That's why she knew that thin places are not only real. They are also part of our everyday reality.

In fact, because my mother believed she could rely on God's merciful presence in thin places, she decided to do something that everyone around her said was unthinkable—if not impossible. She risked her life, against all odds, to birth another child. That was particularly fortunate for me. For if she hadn't, I would never have been born.

PART II

What Makes a Place Thin?
The Five Ws

Chapter 3

Who Am I? Born of Divine Breath

We are not only born from our mother's womb. We are also born of God's breath.

How is it possible to experience the nearness of God in miraculous places of thinness between this world and the next? It can happen because of five Ws: *who, what, where, when,* and *why* we are—and *who* God is. In fact, it's because of the second *who* that I am here.

The story of my birth begins years before I was born—in the midst of a matter of life and death.

It was a cold day in January when my sister, Eileen, came into the world—colder still for a "blue baby" (as the doctors called her), who hadn't turned blue because of the cold. Rather, she had been born with a heart defect that, at the time, was inoperable. My mother, who had given birth to my brother two years before, was devastated. She had prayed to have a daughter this time, only to watch in agony as her fragile newborn straddled the border between life and death day after day, week after week.

Each morning my mother would call the hospital, not knowing if Eileen would still be alive. Each morning she would fall to her knees, thanking God that her baby had been given another day. Six weeks passed before she received the phone call she had been praying for. "Mrs. Rose, Eileen is doing so much better now," the nurse told her. "You can pick her up tomorrow." My mother hung up the phone, weeping tears of joy. She was so elated that she hardly knew what to do first. Then an idea flashed in her mind. She would run down to the store and buy her new daughter that little pink outfit she had admired so many times in Woolworth's window. Almost before she could catch her breath, she was out the door and in the store, purchasing the pretty little outfit while proudly telling everyone within earshot of the miracle that had occurred.

The next day, before leaving for the hospital to pick up Eileen, my mother sat admiring the precious garment, imagining how her new daughter would look in it. Folding it carefully before placing it back in the bag, she paused to thank God for blessing her so richly.

As she made her way to the door, the bag from Woolworth's in one hand, her husband's hand in the other, she thought she heard the phone ring. "I'll take it later," she said to my father, not wanting to delay the homecoming for another minute. The phone stopped ringing, only to ring again a moment later. Hesitantly, she turned around, freeing her hand from her husband's grip to run to the phone.

"Mrs. Rose?" the voice inquired. "Yes?" my mother answered, out of breath. "This is the hospital. I'm sorry but . . ." The rest of the words were a blur. My mother shrieked. The bag from Woolworth's slipped from her trembling hands, spilling the pretty pink outfit onto the floor.

That was where it could have stayed for a lifetime. For, only days before, my mother had been told that because of complications from childbirth, she could never have another child.

Every year on my birthday, my mother told me this sad story—only with a happy ending. "You see, Beverly," she would say. "Against all odds—and against the advice of some pretty distinguished doctors—I had you! That's how much I love you." When I was young, I thought I understood it perfectly. My mother had to have another child, no matter what, even if she had to face death to do it. What mother would want to be stuck for life with only my annoying brother?

Years later, I realized the real reason. My mother had risked her life to birth me because she believed that in that thin place of childbirth, on the border between life and death, this world and the next, God would not only deliver her child, he would also deliver her. She had counted on his life-sustaining breath to keep her alive, while he breathed life into me.

The awesome God who takes our breath away is indeed breath giving. As it says in Genesis, in the beginning, "the Lord God formed the man from the dust of the ground and breathed into his nostrils the breath of life, and the man became a living being" (2:7). God's breath is not only all around us but also within us. It is because of my mother's steadfast belief in God's life-giving breath that I breathe today.

The amazing circumstances of my birth may be why my mother always delighted in not only reliving my own creation story with me again and again but also retelling the original one: "In the beginning God created the heavens and the earth" (Genesis 1:1), she would say dramatically, savoring every moment. "And God said, 'Let there be light,' and there was light" (1:3).

I was so intrigued by the first verses of Genesis that when I was eight years old, I wrote an essay about them. Little did I know at the time that my mother would think my creation was almost as monumental as the Lord's—and that she would share it with everyone she met. In fact, she recited my essay to unsuspecting company so many times that after a while they not only began to suspect but expect.

My mother knew better than to impose her recitation upon newly arrived guests, however. She would wait until there was an opening—which for my mother could be as wide as the Mississippi River. Any mention of children, school, or life in general provoked her exclamation, "That reminds me of something Beverly wrote"—as if she could ever forget. She would clear her throat and start reverently reciting the precious words, which she had long since committed to memory: "On the first day God created heaven and earth," she would begin, pausing to scan the room. Satisfied that her audience was captivated (or at least captive), she would continue reciting my second grade sentences through the sixth day, then pause again, waiting just long enough for expectation to build before reaching the punch line. Then with a twinkle in her eye she would announce, "Then Beverly wrote, 'On the seventh day, God was so tired from all that work that he had to rest.'" The suspecting and expecting company would laugh politely every time—maybe because they were just happy it was over and grateful that I was too young to have, as yet, penned my version of *War and Peace*.

My mother never knew that I hadn't intended my essay to be funny. Even if she had known, I doubt it would have mattered much to her. What she was most proud of was not so much my essay but that I was learning the Bible—and discovering in those holy pages that I am not only God breathed but that I can also experience his breath in miraculous places of thinness. That's why one of the stories she most loved to tell me was of Moses' encounter with God.

I was recently reminded of Moses' amazing meeting with the Lord during a phone call with my good friend Pastor Dave, who informed me that the night before, his van had caught fire and exploded in his driveway. Surprisingly, he didn't seem particularly upset. "It was an old van anyway," he explained. "Maybe God caused it to catch on fire because it was getting too dangerous to drive." Jokingly, I replied, "Or maybe the Lord was aiming for the bush next to the van and missed!"

According to my mother, God didn't miss on that fateful day when Moses was tending his flock and the Lord spoke to him out of a burning bush. When Moses immediately questioned God's choice of him as spokesperson and leader of the Israelites, true to Jewish tradition, it became not a divine monologue but more of a debate. My mother, who like a good Jew always encouraged me to question, proudly related how, at one point, Moses even boldly asked God for a name to tell the people. God answered, "Ehyeh Asher Ehyeh," which means "I am that I am" or "I shall be what I shall be." This name is never mentioned in the Torah again, nor does Moses reveal it to the Jewish people.

For years I wondered about that mysterious reply. One of many interpretations is that a true experience of

God is by definition very private. To each person God will be what he will be, and he cannot be adequately described to anyone else.

That's why the revelation at Mount Sinai is unique in biblical history, for it was the only time God is said to have revealed himself to an entire people. Palpable experiences of God are usually solitary encounters. So why did God choose to manifest himself to the multitudes at Sinai? Kushner offers an explanation suggested by Jewish philosopher and theologian Martin Buber: "At Sinai, the Israelites came into the presence of God in an intense, immediate way and, as a result of that meeting, understood how human beings are meant to live, with a clarity that they had never had before."[1] Whatever God's intentions, those remarkable moments at Sinai have reverberated throughout successive generations, allowing Jews to trace their roots back to people who actually heard God speak. I was a fortunate inheritor not only of the covenant but also of my mother's spirited retelling of the story.

Was the revelation on Mount Sinai an actual face-to-face rendezvous with the living God? Absolutely not. God makes this clear in a subsequent meeting with Moses. When Moses, in an apparent attempt to know God better and thus persuade his people not to worship idols such as the golden calf, asks of God, "Now show me your glory" (Exodus 33:18), God replies, "You cannot see my face, for no one may see me and live" (verse 20). The Lord then takes great pains to spare Moses such a fate. He asks Moses to stand on a nearby rock and directs, "When my glory passes by, I will put you in a cleft in the rock and cover you with my hand until I have passed by. Then I will remove my hand and you will see my back; but my face must not be seen" (verses 22-23). It would not be until the coming of Jesus that the face of God would be revealed, creating the thinnest of all places on the earth.

Pointing the way to Jesus was the prophet Elijah. My mother told me the story of Elijah's amazing departure from the earth not only because she wanted me to know that I am born of God and could have amazing encounters with him but also that I would hopefully return to him—somewhat less dramatically, of course.

> *It would not be until the coming of Jesus that the face of God would be revealed, creating the thinnest of all places on the earth.*

In the Bible, whirlwinds as well as fire are often associated with the presence of the Lord. God appeared to Job out of a storm (see Job 38:1; 40:6). The prophet Isaiah predicted, "Suddenly, in an instant, the Lord Almighty will come with thunder and earthquake and great noise, with windstorm and tempest and flames of a devouring fire" (Isaiah 29:5-6). On the day of Pentecost, wind and fire accompanied the coming of the Holy Spirit (see Acts 2:2-3). Many spectacular sights may herald the Lord's coming, but Elijah made one of the most extraordinary exits: in a chariot of fire.

When Elijah reached the end of his ministry, we find him walking toward the Jordan River with Elisha. As they approached the water, Elijah struck the current with his rolled-up cloak and the waters parted, enabling the two to walk across on dry land. Knowing he was about to depart, Elijah asked Elisha if there was anything he could do for him. Elisha, having witnessed the miracle that had just taken place, responded by asking Elijah for

a double share of Elijah's spirit. In those times, the eldest
son received a double share of the inheritance (see Deuteronomy 21:17). Elisha was asking not for property,
however, but for the power of God. Elijah replied, "If you
see me when I am taken from you, it will be yours—otherwise not" (2 Kings 2:10). Suddenly a chariot of fire and
horses of fire descended, lifting Elijah heavenward in a
whirlwind. Elisha cried out, "My father! My father! The
chariots and horsemen of Israel!" (2 Kings 2:12). Then
Elijah was gone, leaving behind only his cloak. Elisha tore
his clothes in mourning, took the cloak left behind by Elijah, and struck the Jordan with it. The waters parted. A
remarkable transition occurred, as Elijah's power trans-
ferred to Elisha. Yet even more miraculous was that in
that time and place where the river met the shore, on the
boundary between this life and the next, God was
revealed, escorting his beloved prophet to the next world.

The importance of this event cannot be overempha-
sized. According to the Talmud, of all things in the universe made by God, death is the strongest and cannot be
overcome, because death
has been brought about by
sin. Jewish scholars assert,
"If a man tells you that had
Adam not sinned and eaten
of the forbidden tree, he
would have lived for ever,
answer him that actually happened with Elijah."[2] Though
Elijah was not sinless, God gave him the unique and
miraculous honor of bypassing death and entering heaven
directly.

Malachi believed Elijah to be the forerunner of the
Messiah (see Malachi 4:5). Christians believe this minis-

> Even more miraculous was that in that time and place where the river met the shore, on the boundary between this life and the next, God was revealed.

try was fulfilled in the work of John the Baptist (see Mark 9:11-13). Interestingly, Elijah would reappear in the New Testament, along with Moses, during the Transfiguration of Jesus Christ.

Because of Elijah's dramatic exit from this earth, he has entered Jewish folk tradition. Elijah is believed to attend each Passover seder and serve as the savior of poor and oppressed Jews. What Jewish child has not anxiously awaited the moment in the Passover seder when the door is opened for the arrival of Elijah? Every year there is renewed hope that maybe this time he will actually show up in the flesh. It is a tense moment as the door opens and all eyes strain, hoping to get a glimpse of the venerated prophet.

One year, as my parents and I sat with bated breath, my teenage brother breezed back into the room after an unscheduled visit to the bathroom. Seeing the door ajar and no sign of Elijah, he sneered, "Isn't this wearing a little thin?" So were my mother's nerves. I made a mental note never to invite my thick brother to thin places—long before I knew them as such.

Because of my Jewish mother's valiant efforts to teach me about encounters with God, I could experience God's breath in thin places all around me, and know that it was because I was made from his breath—during a most amazing birth. For we are not only born from our mother's womb. We are also born of God's breath. It's because of *who* we are—God's beloved children—that we can draw near to our Father in incredible places of thinness.

Yet my mother taught me even more than who I am. She also taught me *when* I am.

Chapter 4

When Am I? Eternity in Time

We are not only present. We also are eternal.

My mother believed that no matter what happened, God would always be with us in this life. Whether he would always be with us after this life was another matter. That depended on if we were good enough to get to that place of eternal bliss. She considered it her duty to help ensure that my brother and I got to heaven one way or another— or God help us. For she knew *when* we are: We are not only present. We are also eternal.

It has been said that if every synagogue were to disappear from the face of the earth, Jewish religious life would survive intact, sustained in the home. But if Jews were to rely solely on synagogues for their religious life, Jewish commitment would not last for more than a generation.

The Jewish home of my childhood was indeed a religious sanctuary—that is, when my often mischievous brother didn't turn it into a circus. Or when my atheist father, whom my mother enlisted as master of ceremonies on Jewish holidays, didn't unceremoniously pull the plug. My father believed that Jewish rituals needed to be mercifully cut short or they would go on forever. To him, the eternal flame hanging in front of the ark containing the sacred scrolls in the synagogue was not a symbol of the continuity of Jewish tradition and God's eternal presence but of how long the service lasted.

How my mother managed to bring us to so many sacred places was a miracle in itself, especially since it was not only her family but also the demands of the family business in Brooklyn that threatened to derail religious observances. Many lower–middle-class Jews who owned stores, as my parents did, could not afford to close their businesses early. Neither could my parents. But my mother always tried to find a way to comply with Jewish law in this world—so that our souls would make it to the next.

How did she know there is a world to come? There is an ancient Jewish legend in which God speaks to the children of Israel, promising that if they follow the precepts laid down in the Torah, he will grant them a special gift: the gift of the world to come. With great excitement and anticipation, they inquire, "Lord, what is the world to come like?" God answers, "I have already granted you a taste of the world to come. It is the Sabbath."

The Sabbath has been described in many ways: a refuge, a fortress, a palace. I would describe it as a thin place—a place in this world, yet not of it, between this life and the next. In fact, it is said that on the Sabbath the veil between this world and the next is so thin that angels come to earth to bring blessings of peace. To welcome these heavenly guests at the Sabbath table, families sing "Shalom Aleichem," a song inspired by Talmudic legend.

Tradition also says that God sends an extra soul to each one of us at the beginning of the Sabbath so that we can better savor the holiday. One can only marvel at such a place of amazing thinness, where angels and extra souls break through from the next world to this one to be present among us and to give us a taste of eternity.

Jewish scholar and theologian Abraham Heschel writes, "The Sabbath is more than a day, more than a name for a seventh part of the week. It is eternity within time."[1] Interestingly, the Jewish conception of paradise is also a time—the messianic age—in which it will always be Shabbat (the Hebrew word for Sabbath).

It is said that on the Sabbath the veil between this world and the next is so thin that angels come to earth to bring blessings of peace.

Jews need not wait for that time to arrive, however, for the Sabbath allows them to experience a precious moment of paradise while still in this world.

My mother taught us that on the Sabbath we could gain a taste of the next world if we focus on what's right with this one. We should act as if the world had already been redeemed, while working to redeem our own lives by making peace, practicing reconciliation, and extending loving-kindness. She said that the whole world would be redeemed if everyone on earth were to observe two consecutive Sabbaths.

My mother also taught us that the Sabbath has kept Israel more than Israel has kept the Sabbath. Jews may suffer in this life, she would say with a sigh. But even in the midst of anguish and external strife, they can take refuge in the Sabbath, finding internal well-being and peace in a God who is so palpably present—in thin places.

No one knew this better than my mother, who grew up suffering in dire poverty on the Lower East Side of New York. As she witnessed her father, a poor pushcart peddler, labor hard to sell fruits and vegetables to provide for his perpetually hungry family, she knew that his six long, grueling days of work were a means to an end. For on the seventh day, the family could reap the riches of the Sabbath—when time became a delight, sorrow turned to joy, and paupers became kings. Even the poorest and most lowly of workers could enter the presence of God, reclaiming the divine right to dignity, as the distinctions between rich and poor, success and failure vanished, and every person was royalty. As a child, my mother would eagerly await the coming of Sabbath, knowing that it was not only the most sacred day of the week but also of the year.

In fact, the Sabbath is considered so sacred that all of Jewish life and time revolve around it. It can even be considered more important than the High Holy Day of Yom Kippur. Excommunication is the penalty for desecrating Yom Kippur (see Leviticus 23:29-30), but for the Sabbath it is death (see Exodus 31:15). Not even weddings or funerals are allowed to take place on the Sabbath. To understand just how important the Sabbath is, one need only read the Ten Commandments. It is the only day of Jewish observance listed. God commanded the Jewish people first to keep the Sabbath holy and second to observe it (see Exodus 20:8 and Deuteronomy 5:12).

How do Jews observe the Sabbath? The earliest mention of observance is in the Old Testament. At that time, the Jews were instructed to gather a double portion of manna on the sixth day so they did not have to work to gather it on the seventh day (see Exodus 16:29-30). Since then, its observance has changed over time and varies among Jews living in different places. One thing is universal, however. Jews celebrate the world God created in six days because God pronounced it "good," and they rest on the seventh day because God rested on that day—and made it holy.

Universal, that is, except in our household, where the Sabbath was celebrated on Friday night only. That's because Saturday was a day of work, due to the demands of the family business, a children's and ladies' wear store in Brooklyn. My mother succumbed reluctantly to this brutal reality because of the necessity of providing for her struggling family. My father, on the other hand, succumbed to it gleefully. He had a hard enough time just getting through Friday night observances. On the Sabbath, Jews may celebrate a day of rest, yet they refer to it actively by saying they "make Shabbat." My father actively tried to do as little as possible. Families often discuss the weekly Torah portion at Friday dinner, believing that when words of the Torah are said at the table, God is present. Or they may reflect on the week past. Some eat early to attend services, while others sit and talk leisurely at the table. Some attend Saturday services at the temple. Others don't. Some families sing songs after the Sabbath meal. We never got that far. According to my father, once you finished the chicken, Sabbath was over.

I always wished that our Sabbath could have been enriched by such traditions, but I realized the monumental victory my mother won every Friday night just to get my father to sit through the poultry.

What I had hoped for even more was that my family would come together at the end of Sabbath to mark the close of the holiday. My parents were never home from the store on time because Saturday was the busiest day of the week, and they could not afford to close early. That was unfortunate, for the ending of Shabbat is a beautiful and spiritual time in which a Jew can reach a wondrous place. I know, because I participated in the Havdalah ceremony when I attended a Zionist camp as a teenager.

In Hebrew, *havdalah* means "separation." The beauty of Havdalah is that it marks the end of the Sabbath with symbols that signify the transition from the holy to the mundane, from sanctified time to ordinary time. I'll never forget the privilege of participating in this time-honored ceremony every Saturday night at camp.

The Havdalah ceremony begins when three stars are visible in the sky, signifying that the Sabbath is officially over. A candle is lit and blessings are recited over the wine, spices, and fire. Since Havdalah not only ends the Sabbath but also begins the new week, a prayer of thanks for light is said because God started the first week with light. Then a blessing is said to thank God for creation and for distinctions—the distinctions that separate our place in the universe.

Perhaps one of the most beautiful and poignant moments is when the hand holding the candle is cupped, so that the glow of the flame casts a shadow on the palm, a reminder of the contrast between darkness and light.

Before the wine is sipped, some is spilled into a tray. This symbolizes a wish for an abundant week ahead, as well as the sadness that the end of Shabbat brings. The spices are present to raise our spirits and quell the sadness. Some also say that they are there to revive us after the extra soul we have acquired on the Sabbath (to help us better savor the beauty of the holiday) has departed. Whatever one believes, it is inevitably a tearful time.

Every Jew longs for a never-ending, eternal Shabbat ushered in by the Messiah. In fact, because Talmudic legend says that Elijah will come after Havdalah, Jews sing "Eliyahu Hanavi."

My mother, who was of Russian descent, once told me that at the end of Havdalah many Russians serve liquor instead of wine, setting it on fire to represent departing Sabbath angels. More common is to lower the burning candle into the wine to conclude the ceremony before wishing everyone "Shavua tov"—a good week.

Leaving the thin places of the Sabbath is not easy. Yet for the believing Jew, one can return to them not just on Sabbath but on a daily basis through performing *mitzvoth* (plural of mitzvah)—sacred acts done in agreement with God's will. Abraham Heschel asserts, "The Sabbath, as experienced by man, cannot survive in exile, a lonely stranger among days of profanity. It needs the companionship of the other days. All days of the week must be spiritually consistent with the seventh day."[2] One way Jews achieve such spiritual consistency is to perform mitzvoth. They believe those mitzvoth can eventually earn them a place in heaven, where it will forever be Shabbat.

My mother, ever mindful of my soul making it to heaven, taught me that the Jew is commanded to be aware of the opportunity to do mitzvoth every moment of every day, not just in making Shabbat, which is itself a mitzvah. As is studying the Torah, which is said to be equivalent to all mitzvoth combined. In fact, next to Torah, the concept of mitzvah is the most basic to the life of a Jew, as central to Jewish consciousness as the concept of salvation is to the Christian. According to Bar Kapparah, a third-century rabbi, "Greater are the good deeds of the righteous men than all the creation of heaven and earth."³

What comprises a mitzvah? The word means everything from God's specific commandments (there are 613 of them, although few Jews obey all of them), to the body of law itself, to our obligation to fulfill the law, to the act of fulfilling the law or our obligations under it. In essence, a mitzvah is everything associated with doing what God requires of us—and more. It connotes goodness, virtue, and holiness, because by choosing to do good in performing a mitzvah, one encounters the Divine.

As Abraham Heschel puts it, "Holiness is not exclusively the product of the soul but the outcome of moments in which God and soul meet in the light of a good deed."⁴ The ideal Jewish life is to perform a string of mitzvoth every day, thereby discovering the sacred in the mundane and finding oneself with God in a thin place.

My mother taught me about mitzvoth not only by example but also by giving me an example from her childhood—in reverse: her legendary chocolate story. She would begin by telling me about her neighbor "Fat Kid" (that was his name, apparently), who would often ask her to accompany him to the candy store to buy a piece of candy. My mother's parents were much too poor to provide their children with such treats, so she would eagerly consent to join him, hoping that she would receive a piece of the precious chocolate. As they walked, side by side, block after block, she would begin to salivate in anticipation of the sugary treat. But when they arrived and "Fat Kid" paid his nickel for the chocolate morsel, he would proceed to gulp down every last bit. He never gave my mother one single bite. "It would have been a mitzvah for

'Fat Kid' to offer me a piece of chocolate," my mother would explain, still teary eyed as she relived the painful deprivation in the retelling. "And a greater mitzvah for him," she would add, "for he was being given the opportunity to do a good deed." As a child listening to her story, I secretly believed that the greatest mitzvah of all would have been for "Fat Kid" to give away all his candy so he wouldn't have been so fat. Unfortunately he never had any intention of doing so.

Not that the intention to do good is required, nor is understanding the deed. When the Israelites were given the Torah, their response was, "We will do everything the Lord has said; we will obey" (Exodus 24:7). In doing mitzvoth, one must act first and understand afterward. This applies even to giving charity.

In Hebrew, the word for charity is *tzedakah*. Jewish philanthropy was born out of the belief that what we possess really belongs to God. It merely passes through our hands during the brief moments of our lives. Giving money to the poor is a tradition practiced during nearly all Jewish celebrations. On the Sabbath, for example, it was common practice for my grandmother to put aside money in a charity box before the candles were lit. Jews are encouraged to give, regardless of motive—even for the wrong reasons. It is hoped that eventually the act of giving itself will lead them to give for the right reason next time. It is questionable whether everyone is salvageable, however. Such is the case with the character in Isaac Asimov's story: "The rich Mr. Goldberg was brooding one day. Finally he muttered to himself: 'What good are my steamship lines to me; my oil stock; my department-store chain; all my hundreds of millions of dollars—when my poor mother is starving in an attic?'"[5] As my mother would say, these are not the words of a good bar mitzvah boy.

What does a "bar mitzvah boy" have to do with performing mitzvoth? Actually, just about everything. The term *bar mitzvah* refers to a boy who has become sufficiently adult to be expected to take mitzvoth to heart and be held accountable for them. The girl is called a *bat mitzvah*. The bar or bat mitzvah ceremonies commemorate that moment in time when the boy or girl becomes a member of the segment of believing Jews who live a life of performing mitzvoth, not out of obligation, duty, or personal gain, but for the sake of the sacred act itself.

I never became a bat mitzvah. My father gave me a choice between Hebrew school and clarinet lessons. Let's just say that the thought of spending hours in Hebrew school was not music to my ears. Besides, I believed that my mother could teach me all I needed to know about Judaism. Jazz clarinet she couldn't teach me.

There is no doubt that becoming a bat mitzvah would have had an impact on my life. Yet attending my brother's bar mitzvah left a far greater impact on me than anyone could have imagined—precisely because of the thin place that did *not* materialize in front of my eyes.

I was nine years old when I attended my brother's bar mitzvah. He was thirteen and about to celebrate the day he became a man. Unfortunately the man he would become didn't show up until he was thirty. Nevertheless, we celebrated anyway.

It was by far the most anticipated family affair in years and the most agonizingly planned. Every detail had to be perfect—and for some reason, lavender.

When the day finally arrived, our family and a hundred of our closest friends and neighbors crowded the temple to overflowing in anticipation of my brother's squeaking the Haftarah reading from the pulpit—and the free stuffed derma and knishes that awaited them when the painful process was over.

When the service finally ended and the guests were storming the smorgasbord, I went looking for my mother, who was nowhere to be found. Someone directed me to the reception room, where dinner was about to be served. I imagined my mother was there to make a final check that all the lavenders matched.

As I opened the door where the reception was about to be held, I gasped at the beauty of the decor. My mother, her back turned to me, was gasping as well, her shoulders heaving up and down. "Mom," I whispered, as she turned around to face me, teary eyed, "what's the matter?" I assumed she was overcome by the beauty of the setting. She was overwhelmed all right, but by something she would never overcome. For she had just been informed that her mother, who was uncharacteristically late for such an important occasion, was not coming at all. She had broken her hip and had been rushed to the hospital.

My mother was shattered. She had waited her whole life for the bittersweet moment when her mother, a refugee from czarist Russia, would experience the fulfillment of her dreams in seeing her oldest grandson become a bar mitzvah. Now it would only be a bitter moment, not only for my grandmother, but also for my mother, who having experienced so much deprivation in her life, was being cruelly deprived again.

My mother stared past me with a faraway look as she wiped her eyes. It was the same otherworldly look I had witnessed on Shabbat, but this time she was in a far different place. The well of unspeakable suffering deep within my mother's heart had suddenly bubbled to the surface, threatening to drown us both. The tears in her eyes seemed to have extinguished the Light.

Where is God now? I desperately wondered in that thin place of suffering. *That unknowable God my mother believes is always with us in good times as well as bad? Is it conceivable that he's not always here with us? If he isn't, how can he see the good deeds we do? If he doesn't, how can we ever get to heaven? Or are we doomed to be present without a promising future?*

If we are doomed, I continued to muse, *then why on the Sabbath did God give us a taste of the world to come? Why does he encourage us to do mitzvoth so that we may be rewarded with heaven? My mother says that God gave us an immortal soul. We are not only present. We are also eternal. So why wouldn't he be present to see the good we do, so that we may have a future in paradise?*

Then one day, disabled by disease and disillusioned by life, I caught more than just a glimpse of the answer—the Answerer actually appeared. In that miraculous moment, getting to that place of eternal bliss was no longer only a hope. It became a promise.

In that miraculous moment, getting to that place of eternal bliss was no longer only a hope. It became a promise.

Chapter 5

Who Is God? The Unknowable Made Knowable

God is not only the Father. He is also the Son.

On the day of my brother's bar mitzvah, I witnessed my despairing mother momentarily lose hope in God. It was then that I first began to wonder: *Who* is the God I had glimpsed in the eyes of my mother and in amazing places all around me?

Such a weighty question quickly faded, however, in the continuing wonders of childhood experiences in thin places. By the time I reached adulthood, I had forgotten the question altogether. Thrust into the thick of things in an adult world, I learned to cope well enough on my own. I had a good life, a successful career, and a bright future. I could even live with troubling cosmic questions—as long as the cosmos was generally aligned in my favor. Not that I wouldn't have welcomed a sign from God once in a while, just for reassurance, but it would have had to be a very palpable one.

Children may think more concretely than adults, but when it comes to things of the Spirit, adults often ask for more concrete signs. "If only God would give me some clear sign!" comedian Woody Allen remarks. "Like making a large deposit in my name at a Swiss bank."[1] Whether or not we share his wish for wealth, most of us can relate to Allen's desire for a visible sign from God.

What if one morning that sign came? What if we awakened to find a fat bankbook lying on the night table with a note that read, "Do you believe me now?" Would we?

In our time, such a miracle seems nearly impossible. God's appearance at Mount Sinai may have been burned into the collective consciousness of Jews for time immemorial. But no Jew has seen a burning bush lately. Such an amazing affirmation of divine presence undoubtedly left the ancient Hebrews gaping in awe, but modern-day Jews have been left doubting, groping for glimpses.

Today's Christians face a somewhat similar dilemma. Unlike their first-century counterparts, who had the privilege of communing with Jesus in the flesh, twenty-first-century Christians are left to relate to a risen Christ.

It wouldn't be so bad if as adults we could believe what as children we didn't need to see. But unfortunately, as adults we may spend far more time wondering why God isn't showing up than we did as children in wonder that he did. As Abraham Heschel writes, because of indifference or the demands of daily routine, "the perception of the glory is a rare occurrence in our lives. We fail to wonder, we fail to respond to the presence. This is the tragedy of every man."[2] Maybe that's why Jesus said, "Let the little children come to me, and do not hinder them, for the kingdom of God belongs to such as these. I tell you the truth, anyone who will not receive the kingdom of God like a little child will never enter it" (Mark 10:14-15).

Why do so many adults need to see before they can believe? Maybe it's because many of us have seen too much—particularly when it comes to suffering. Inexplicable suffering can shake the very foundations of faith. I know, because that's what happened to me— when I inexplicably became the sufferer. Stricken with a neuromuscular disease in the prime of my life, at the height of my career as a clinical psychologist, my questions about God resurfaced more urgently than ever. When the material world failed me, God was no longer immaterial. When suffering became personal, I needed a God who was up close and personal. Childhood impressions were no longer enough. I needed positive proof.

It's not as if I hadn't been exposed to suffering all my life. It's just that it had never seriously challenged my very belief in God. Growing up Jewish, I had been well acquainted with the darkness born of suffering in my mother's eyes that stemmed from the horrors of Jewish history. My mother wasn't alone. Our ancestors had roamed in the darkness for thousands of years, too often feeling God's absence rather than his presence when they needed him most. Yet that didn't necessarily cause them to lose faith.

Throughout history, Jews have tried to be optimistic, looking forward to the day the Messiah would come. Jews today eagerly await the time when the horrors of persecution and genocide, such as the pogroms in czarist Russia, the Holocaust, and the bitter conflict in Israel, will be things of the past. Yet they fear it might not be for a very long time, as evidenced by the following story:

In a small Russian shtetl, the community council decides to pay a poor Jew a ruble a week to sit at the town's entrance and be the first to greet the Messiah when he arrives. The man's brother comes to see him, and is puzzled why he took such a low-paying job. "It's true," the poor man responds, "the pay is low. But it's a steady job."[3]

Jews pray for the day that the Messiah will come, hopefully sooner rather than later. In that blessed day, the calf and the lion will lie down together, Isaiah said. But for now, quips Woody Allen, "The lion and the calf shall lie down together but the calf won't get much sleep."[4]

My mother managed to keep her faith in God, even though the source of the darkness lurking in her eyes— even on the brightest of occasions—was the horrific moment in human history when multitudes perished and lives were shattered for generations in brutal pogroms in Eastern Europe. I grew up in the shadow of those murders, even though they took place decades before I was born.

What happened to my relatives during the pogroms in the early twentieth century was a closely guarded secret in my family. My grandmother spoke little of her experiences in czarist Russia. Even if she had, I wouldn't have understood. Nor comprehended, for she spoke mostly Russian and Yiddish. Such stories, even retold in English, would have lost something in the translation.

Only years later, when I researched the pogroms for myself, did I begin to grasp the enormity of the perils my grandparents had faced when Russian mobs attacked Jews, murdering men, women, and children and destroying their property. The anti-Semitic policy of the government and its reluctance to stop the attacks only served to perpetuate the violence. Almost all my maternal relatives were killed in those pogroms. My grandparents fled to

America in 1914 while my grandmother was pregnant with my mother, which made travel so much more difficult. Yet even more agonizing was her brother's refusal to leave Russia. Eventually he, too, escaped to America, but he returned homesick to his native land shortly thereafter. Tragically, he was brutally murdered.

My grandparents were poor in Russia. Nevertheless, my grandfather had earned the distinction of being the only high school graduate in his village, which elevated his status and his hopes. All that vanished, however, when he and my grandmother escaped Russia, leaving almost everything behind, including their dreams. Sadly, rather than finding even greater opportunities in the New World, they found themselves living in a ghetto on the Lower East Side of New York, in some of the most crowded conditions on earth.

In my visits to that ghetto as a child, I glimpsed the enormous deprivation my mother had experienced growing up. Indirectly, she also had become a victim of the pogroms, sharing horrendous poverty with her struggling parents. While my mother had told me little about the perils of her upbringing, the dark, dank, cockroach-infested apartment where my mother had suffered in silence for years spoke volumes.

By the time I visited, long after my grandfather's death, the condition of the apartment had deteriorated even more than when my mother had lived there—as had my grandmother's health. It was an eerie interplay of the animate and the inanimate falling victim to the ravages of time. As I stood in that place that time *didn't* forget, it seemed that time had actually stood still, trapping the anguished inhabitant forever. Or was she as trapped as she seemed?

If you looked closely, just beyond the clutter that seemed permanently affixed to the countertop, you would come upon an incongruous sight—my grandmother's recently polished brass candlesticks. Apparently, even in that seemingly God-forsaken place, my grandmother regularly prayed, holding on to faith in the midst of horrific suffering. Even today, I can picture her standing alone in that dilapidated kitchen lighting the candles week after week on the Sabbath, steadying her shaking hands, propping up her weak body, mustering the little energy she had left to reach out to God. In a life buried in darkness, did she somehow manage to unearth an unknowable God who was waiting for her at the border between a fallen and a flawless world? Whether she did or didn't, how she managed to keep her faith in an invisible, inconceivable, and apparently indifferent God week after week in the midst of such suffering is still a mystery to me.

When I began to study the Holocaust as a teenager, I first gained a glimpse of the magnitude of suffering borne of rampant anti-Semitism. My family may not have been directly involved in Hitler's murderous scheme, but I was powerfully affected when I attended Zionist camp and learned the gruesome facts. Several years later, when I visited Yad Vashem, the Holocaust memorial in Israel, it all became frighteningly real.

I will never forget the somber day I entered the Hall of Remembrance on the grounds of Yad Vashem, which was created by the Israeli Knesset to preserve the memory of the 6 million Jewish victims of the Holocaust. If ever there were a place where I experienced the presence of God, it was on that sacred ground. My visit took place over thirty years ago, but the memory of the thinness of that place forever burns in my heart.

Who Is God? The Unknowable Made Knowable

Upon entering a darkened hall, my eyes were immediately drawn to a memorial flame casting shadows on a crypt containing ashes of victims. On the floor were names of Nazi concentration camps where millions had perished. In the hushed silence of that very thin place, I heard faint murmurs of the mourner's kaddish (prayers for the dead), which grew louder and louder, overwhelming me in a crushing wave of sorrow. Suddenly a piercing shriek rang out as a woman, hysterical from grief, began clawing her way through the crowd to the door. Had she been a victim of the camps?

I would never know, but I would come to know one victim's story quite well, when a shy man of slim build made his way to a podium at Boston University in the early 1980s and uttered softly into the microphone, "My name is Elie Wiesel." Seated in the balcony, I leaned forward in eager anticipation of his words, for I knew his name well. He was a world-renowned survivor of the Holocaust, a voice of conscience for the entire world.

I learned far more about suffering that day than I did about thin places. While Wiesel spoke on behalf of millions of victims of Nazi atrocities committed against him and his people, he refused to speak for God. That's because during the horrors of the Holocaust Wiesel had waited and waited—in vain—for God to speak for himself.

Elie was only fifteen years old when he and his family were deported to Auschwitz by the Nazis. He and his two older sisters survived, but his mother and younger sister perished. Elie was later transported to Buchenwald with his father, who perished just before the liberation of the camp in 1945.

The stories Wiesel tells about his internment echo the

47

pained voices of millions who suffered and died. Daily life included brutality, starvation, and despair. In his book *Night*, Wiesel vividly describes the horrors of the first night he arrived at a camp and saw black smoke rising from the ovens and smelled the stink of burning human flesh:

Never shall I forget that night, the first night in camp, which has turned my life into one long night, seven times cursed and seven times sealed. Never shall I forget that smoke. Never shall I forget the little faces of the children, whose bodies I saw turned into wreaths of smoke beneath a silent blue sky.

Never shall I forget those flames which consumed my faith forever.

Never shall I forget that nocturnal silence which deprived me, for all eternity, of the desire to live. Never shall I forget those moments which murdered my God and my soul and turned my dreams to dust. Never shall I forget these things, even if I am condemned to live as long as God Himself. Never.[5]

Tragically, in the horror of the camps, Wiesel could find no border between darkness and light—only perpetual darkness, where the light of God was nowhere to be found. That's when he became an accuser of God for not showing up.

In a speech Wiesel gave in the East Room of the White House in 1999, he lamented, "Rooted in our tradition, some of us felt that to be abandoned by humanity then was not the ultimate. We felt that to be abandoned by God was worse than to be punished by Him. Better an unjust God than an indifferent one. For us to be ignored by God was a harsher punishment than to be a victim of His anger."[6]

One would think that in the dark shadow of such suffering, God's light could be seen even more brightly coming through the veil. Some concentration camp victims did find their way to that transcendent Light. Corrie ten Boom, a Christian interned at Ravensbrück, was one of them. She has said of her experience, "However deep the pit, God's love is deeper still."[7] That is a remarkable statement coming from a woman who witnessed so many people perish in the camps—including her own sister, Betsie. What did she know that Wiesel didn't? Or was it Who? The answer may lie in the death of a child.

It was a child, just a little child, with the face of a sad angel, who was hanged one day in front of thousands of prisoners, Wiesel recalls. "All eyes were on the child. He was lividly pale, almost calm, biting his lips. The gallows threw its shadow over him. . . . For more than half an hour he stayed there, struggling between life and death, dying in slow agony under our eyes. . . . Behind me, I heard . . . 'Where is God now?' And I heard a voice within me answer him: 'Where is He? Here He is—He is hanging here on this gallows.'"[8]

Catholic novelist and moralist François Mauriac, in the foreword to *Night*, struggles to find an answer to Elie's despair. Mauriac poignantly writes, "And I, who believe that God is love, what answer could I give my young questioner, whose dark eyes still held the reflection of that angelic sadness which had appeared one day upon the face of the hanged child? What did I say to him? Did I speak of that other Jew, his brother, who may have resembled him—the Crucified, whose Cross has conquered the world? Did I affirm that the stumbling block to his faith was the cornerstone of mine, and that the conformity between the Cross and the suffering of men was in my eyes the key to that impenetrable mystery whereon the faith of his childhood had perished?"[9]

It was only when my fate was hanging in the balance that I stumbled upon that Cornerstone, who to me had previously been a stumbling block—the suffering one who went to the cross to save this sufferer's life.

I was in the midst of my postdoctoral year at a Harvard-affiliated teaching hospital when I began to develop disabling symptoms. Several years later, too ill to work, I resigned from a lucrative position as an associate director of a regional nursing home program. What had begun as muscle pain and fatigue had developed into a full-blown assault, affecting many vital parts of my body. I found myself bedridden, losing the battle to a progressive, often fatal neuromuscular disease. C. S. Lewis writes, "You never know how much you really believe anything until its truth or falsehood becomes a matter of life and death to you."[10] Finding out who God really is was not just a matter of life and death for me—it was all I had left.

Forced to relinquish my apartment in Boston, which I could no longer afford, I moved in with my parents in Florida. I lay in bed for months with worsening symptoms, bemoaning my fate. Just when I thought it couldn't get any worse, it did. My mother, the person I loved most in the world and my best friend, died three months after I arrived.

To lose her only weeks after I had revived her the day she collapsed right in front of me was a terrible shock. Especially since after she was rushed to the hospital, she successfully underwent open-heart surgery to replace the defective aortic valve that had suddenly closed and almost killed her the week before. No one expected that ten days after surgery she would die from postoperative complications. She had been given a 98 percent chance of survival. She was in the 2 percent. Now I had truly lost everything.

In the dark years after my mother's death, there were no transcendent places—no light at the end of the tunnel—only haunting, unanswerable questions. I spent countless agonizing hours shadowboxing with a seemingly absent, incomprehensible God who appeared to duck whenever I got near. At first I tried to get him off the hook. *Maybe God just doesn't know about my suffering,* I thought. But then how could he be all knowing? *Maybe he just doesn't care.* But then how could he be all loving? *Maybe he is unable to intercede.* Then how could he be all powerful? Then I questioned myself. What had I done to deserve such a horrendous fate? Was it a punishment?

It's not as if I were prepared to personally suffer. I may have learned about the suffering of my ancestors and seen suffering in the eyes of my Jewish mother, but it never directly struck me. Nor did the suffering I witnessed in my practice as a clinical psychologist, although I cared deeply about the wounded souls I encountered. I had spent years walking the halls of a state hospital, treating bedraggled, drooling patients who paced endlessly back and forth, destined for nowhere. I had stood at the bedside of frail nursing home patients who, having given their all to families and friends, were breathing

their last breaths alone. It was agonizing not to be able
to find a way to heal those tragic victims. Yet how could
I, when even the gods of psychology at Harvard didn't
know the answers?

If there were places of transcendence in the midst of
such human suffering, I hadn't experienced them, hard
as I tried. Yet at the end of the day, I was able to live with
the unanswerable questions, if uneasily. *Doesn't everyone suffer one way or another?* I rationalized. Despite
advances in medicine and psychiatry, don't we all hurt
to some degree, if not physically and emotionally, then at
least spiritually? And not just those of us who face overwhelming tragedy, but each and every one of us, at some
level? As philosopher Henry David Thoreau lamented,
"The mass of men lead lives of quiet desperation."[11] Who
was I to figure out the answer to suffering? I was not
alone. Peter Kreeft, professor of philosophy at Boston
College asserts, "Modern man does not have an answer
to the question of why. Our society is the first one that
simply does not give us any answer to the problem of suffering except a thousand means of avoiding it."[12]

I tried to avoid thinking too much about the suffering
I saw all around me because I saw no value in dwelling
on it—nor in suffering itself. Little did I know that dwelling in my own suffering would bring me to a place that
would change the very person I was—and would become.
C. S. Lewis writes, "I have seen great beauty of spirit in
some who were great sufferers. I have seen men, for the
most part, grow better not worse with advancing years,
and I have seen the last illness produce treasures of forti-
tude and meekness from most unpromising subjects. . . .
If the world is indeed a 'vale of soul-making' it seems on
the whole to be doing its work."[13] It would take enor-

mous personal suffering to eventually convince me to
reach out to the maker of souls, who came through the
veil in a thin place to touch my soul—and remake it.

Yet this would not occur before I spent years lying in
bed, suffering the ravages of my devastating disease. Not
before I battled through countless nights calling out to the
universe for answers, feeling cast aside, banished by the
mainstream. Stripped of what I considered to be the most
important things in life—employment, prestige, money, a
lakeside apartment, and even my loving mother—I dan-
gled just above the abyss. I struggled to see form or shape,
but I saw nothing. I screamed, but I heard nothing. For
the first time in my life, I understood how Job must have
felt when he lost everything—his health, his children, his
worldly possessions—and felt abandoned by God. Yet
even when God finally did show up for Job, he did not
immediately restore all the poor man had lost. Nor did he
give Job answers. Rather, God gave him his presence. Was
that the answer? Peter Kreeft tells us, "Like Job, I have
wrestled with God about suffering. . . . I lost. Like Job.
And that is the only possible way to win."[14] Drenched in
the tears of Job, I could not find a way to win—until I met
the Victor himself.

One fateful afternoon when, surrounded by all the
books on world religions I had read, I spied one more. It
was the only one I had purposely not read. I reached for
it, then pulled back. "It is forbidden," I murmured to
myself. "Why did I buy it in the first place? It is blasphemy." Yet what harm could it do? I reasoned. After all,
it's only a book. Finally, out of desperation, I succumbed.
I did the one thing I thought I would never do. I picked
up the book and began reading about the very person my
mother blamed for the murder of my maternal relatives—

the very person she believed had been responsible for the pogroms that had destroyed her family: the person of Jesus Christ.

I expected to find a message of anti-Semitism and hate. Instead I found a Jew who despised hatred. I expected to find a divided God. Instead I found a God of unity. I expected to find Jesus coming between God and me. Instead I found God, in Jesus, coming for me. As I laid the book down, exhausted and in pain, I began to meditate, and for some reason, I whispered the name "Jesus." Suddenly an awesome, loving, peaceful presence came over me. He was more real than any reality I had ever experienced, more true than any truth I had ever known. I knew that God had finally revealed himself to me—in the last place on earth I ever would have expected—in Jesus Christ. In the extraordinary thinness of that place, my questions were finally answered—by the Answerer himself.

Abraham Heschel observes, "There are moments in which, to use a Talmudic phrase, heaven and earth kiss each other; in which there is a lifting of the veil at the horizon of the known, opening a vision of what is eternal in time. . . . The voice of Sinai goes on for ever."[15] If there is meaning in suffering, it is found when, standing on the border between life and death, darkness and light, you call out beyond yourself to that voice of Sinai and amazingly find yourself with God in a miraculous thin place of peace. "He'll come, even through the mist, through the fog, like the light from a lighthouse,"

In the extraordinary thinness of that place, my questions were finally answered—by the Answerer himself.

writes Kreeft. "You'll see him through your tears. That's a promise."[16]

I saw God that fateful day as I lay in my sickbed—the God my mother had believed was always with us. He showed up personally, revealing to me who he really is. God is not only the Father. He is also the Son.

I not only saw him through my tears. I also felt the tears of a suffering God in Jesus—and that has made all the difference.

Chapter 6

Who Is Jesus? God Unveiled

Jesus is not only the embodiment of God himself. He is also the embodiment of God's love and grace.

When suffering became unbearable and I needed to know God personally, I found him in his Son. Jesus came to me in my suffering, just as he came to my ancestors two thousand years ago. Because Jesus came, I could be certain of *who* God is. What I was still not so sure about, however, was whether God really cares.

The Bible tells us that Jesus came in sacrificial love to give his life for us by dying on a cross. He kept company with sinners and with the sick, breaking societal rules to help and heal them. Are those the actions of a God who doesn't care—the indifferent God Elie Wiesel portrays? Or are they efforts of a God who loves us? Peter Kreeft writes, "He came. He entered space and time and suffering. He came, like a lover. Love seeks above all intimacy, presence, togetherness. Not happiness. 'Better unhappy with her than happy without her'—that is the word of a lover. He came. That is the salient fact, the towering truth, that alone keeps us from putting a bullet through our heads. He came."[1]

If Jesus came because he cares, why, at times, is it so hard for me to feel loved by him? Why, as I fall to the floor in a neurological episode, shaking uncontrollably, don't I think to myself, *Don't worry, God loves you.* After all, Jesus came. Why do I expend monumental effort to pick myself up, rather than wait for him to swoop down, take me in his heavenly arms, and place me comfortably in bed to shake safely there—or maybe while he's at it, heal

> Jesus kept company with sinners and with the sick, breaking societal rules to help and heal them.

me? If I believe he is not an absent God and, as my friend Joan claims, is "always sitting in my living room," why don't I wait for him to rise from the sofa and give me a hand? After

all, he has risen from far more difficult places than that. Is he indifferent or just a couch potato? Is he afraid he'll miss the ending of a good TV show? Doesn't he always know how it ends anyway? I have to confess that I get rather frustrated at times having to rise by myself, especially when my episodes are often due to fatigue brought on by writing books about him. If Jesus came in sacrificial love, why at times do I feel as if I'm the one doing the sacrificing?

It was easier to accept God's apparent inaction when I believed he was absent. Now that he came to me, and is very much present in my life, I question why he sits idly by and does nothing. Or does he?

I'm not saying that I don't appreciate the fact that God came. It was the most important moment of my life.

How startling for me, a Jew, to experience in Jesus the palpable presence of the Lord. How amazing that God came to earth in Jesus centuries ago to reveal his face. No Jew of the Old Testament could claim to know God's face, nor survive his gaze. It was veiled, even in the Tabernacle—in the Most Holy Place.

The Tabernacle, a tentlike structure, built based on instructions the Lord gave to Moses, was constructed so that the Israelites could regularly perform sacrifices and acts of worship commanded by the law. Suspended on four supports, it was divided by a curtain into two compartments: the Holy Place and the Most Holy Place, where the Ark of the Covenant, containing the precious tablets of the Law, was kept.

No one dared enter the Most Holy Place, the innermost compartment, for fear of death—except for the high priest on special ceremonial occasions. Performing ritual baths and animal sacrifices and donning special clothing, he entered the Most Holy Place alone and in fear, wearing bells and a rope around his ankle so that he could be pulled out, should the bells fall silent, signaling he had died.

It took none other than Jesus coming through the veil to unveil the face of God and open the path for us into the Most Holy Place, by way of the Cross. According to Luke, "It was now about the sixth hour, and darkness came over the whole land until the ninth hour, for the sun stopped shining. And the curtain of the temple was torn in two. Jesus called out with a loud voice, 'Father, into your hands I commit my spirit.' When he had said this, he breathed his last" (Luke 23:44-46). According to the book of Hebrews, "We have confidence to enter the Most Holy Place by the blood of Jesus, by a new and living way opened for us through the curtain, that is, his body, and since we have a great priest over the house of God, let us draw near to God with a sincere heart in full assurance of faith" (10:19-22).

In casting aside the curtain upon his death, Jesus gave us unrestricted access to God, just as he has unrestricted access to us. We no longer have to be shielded from God's presence in exclusive sacred places, just as we are not shielded from him. God

God can be found anywhere we are, just as he can find us anywhere.

can be found anywhere we are, just as he can find us anywhere. He can reach us at any moment if he chooses to— that is, if he's not too indifferent.

How could God be indifferent if he bothered to come to earth in Jesus? Such an amazing coming was quite a gesture in itself. As journalist and best-selling author Philip Yancey asserts, "In one body, Christ brought the two worlds together, joining spirit and matter at long last, unifying creation in a way that had not been seen since Eden."[2] Besides, Jesus didn't just come. He took on the limitations of his creation. In his desire to do whatever it takes to be with us, he did whatever it took to be one of us. In the process, he exposed himself to us in unprecedented ways.

He allowed us to touch him, crowd him, intrude upon his solitude, even see him cry. Such intimacy between God and his people was unheard of at the time. The ancient Israelites may have been struck dead when they touched the sacred Ark of the Covenant, but first-century Jews could hug God himself. The Israelites may have been forbidden to pronounce or even spell God's name, but first-century Jews could be on a first-name basis with the Son of God and even address his Father as *Abba* or *Daddy*. As Philip Yancey writes, "No other religion—not Judaism, not Hinduism, not Buddhism or Islam—offers this unique contribution of an all-powerful God who willingly takes on the limitations and suffering of his creation."[3] The world has never known a more astonishing breaking through the veil. "God's answer is simply the most incredible event in all of history," says Peter Kreeft. "Eternity entered time. The mind of God, the word of life—timeless, eternal life—became as temporally alive, as jumpingly alive, as a lion."[4] Jesus did not come as a lion, however. He came as a sacrificial lamb. He didn't come to abolish our suffering in this world. He came to suffer and die in this life to assure us of the next one.

An indifferent God would never have reached out to us in such an extraordinary way, and he certainly wouldn't have suffered and died for us. Yet how can we reconcile the fact that Jesus could have rescued first-century Jews from the oppression of Roman occupation but didn't? He could rescue us from our suffering today, but for the most part he doesn't. Apparently it's not because he doesn't love us or is indifferent. After all, he came.

Maybe it's because he doesn't truly understand our suffering. That doesn't seem likely. The Bible tells us that Jesus chose to live in the midst of those everyone else scorned. He came to the sick, the poor, the prostitutes, and the tax collectors. God didn't spare himself suffering. When he came to earth in Jesus, he not only came to comfort and save the suffering, he came to know first-hand what it is like to be a suffering human being—and we saw his response, firsthand.

Jesus wept when his friend Lazarus died. He healed the blind, the lepers, the crippled, while suffering compassionately with them. He did not punish or berate those who suffered by blaming them for their plight. Instead, by grace, he gave them his heart, his powers of healing, and ultimately, his life on a cross. As Philip Yancey observes, "Jesus went out of his way to embrace the unloved and unworthy, the folks who matter not at all to the rest of society—they embarrass us, we wish they'd go away—to prove that even 'nobodies' matter infinitely to God."[5] Jesus allied himself with the people who had been sidelined by life, while the rich and the powerful stood on the sidelines, mocking him because he was nothing like what they expected God to be—even though it is written in the Old Testament: "He had no beauty or majesty to attract us to him, nothing in his appearance that we should desire him. He was despised and rejected by men, a man of sorrows, and familiar with suffering. Like one from whom men hide their faces he was despised, and we esteemed him not" (Isaiah 53:2-3).

Not only did Jesus live among the suffering, but he was also made to suffer for living among them. The powerful elite taunted him for associating with undesirables. They derided him for breaking deeply rooted customs when he touched lepers, who were considered unclean; dined with tax collectors; communed with women; and healed the sick on the Sabbath. Jesus was laughed at, his sanity was questioned, and he was ultimately killed. This does not sound like a God who doesn't understand what it's like to suffer. It is a God who suffered with and for those who suffered.

If Jesus is loving and caring and understands suffering, why didn't he use his powers to heal the masses?

Why doesn't he heal everyone who is sick today? Maybe God is not powerful enough.

That's what Harold Kushner believes. Rabbi Kushner experienced the ultimate in suffering when his three-year-old son was diagnosed with an incurable genetic illness that led to a tragically premature death. The rabbi agonized over why God would allow a bright, innocent child to suffer such a horrible fate. Kushner attributes God's lack of intervention to the Lord's powerlessness. He writes, "Unable to keep my son from dying, God showed me how to redeem his death from being a statistic and forge it into a book that would bring healing to millions."[6] While, Kushner's faith is admirable, I question his conclusion. The God I know, who walked the earth in Jesus, demonstrated conclusively the enormity of his power, even though he was not as interested in demonstrating his power as he was his love. How was his power evidenced? One way was by performing miracles.

The definition of a miracle is an event that causes us to wonder. Jesus' miracles not only caused us to wonder at the miracle but also to wonder why, if he had such powers, he didn't use them to rescue all of humanity. Some might say that the miracles of Jesus were merely a magician's trick. I believe otherwise.

There is a supernatural quality about miracles that distinguishes them from works of magic. Those who perform magic claim the power as their own. But miracles depend upon divine will, not upon the power of the performer, who is merely an agent of God. Miracles can also be distinguished from events in nature that excite wonder. Every blade of grass may be called a miracle, but miracles in Christian usage are generally signs that teach a lesson, revealing an underlying truth. In the days of the

Bible, God often performed miracles in times of waning spirituality, such as during the Exodus, when his people worshipped a golden calf, and at the time of Elijah when people worshipped Baal. When Jesus came, the Jewish leaders were steeped in hypocrisy and self-righteousness. Jesus tells us that his miracles were evidence of the truth of his message and his oneness with the Father. "Why then do you accuse me of blasphemy because I said, 'I am God's Son'? Do not believe me unless I do what my Father does. But if I do it, even though you do not believe me, believe the miracles, that you may know and understand that the Father is in me, and I in the Father" (John 10:36-38). Unfortunately, for the most part, even Jesus' miracles didn't convince the Jewish leaders who was God.

The miracles Jesus performed were not the only evidence of God's power. God's coming to earth in Jesus was nothing short of miraculous. So was the Transfiguration of Jesus, when the Son of God was visibly glorified in front of the very eyes of Peter, James, and John. Luke reports, "The appearance of [Jesus'] face changed, and his clothes became as bright as a flash of lightning" (9:29). Matthew tells us, "His face shone like the sun" (17:2). Mark says, "His clothes became dazzling white, whiter than anyone in the world could bleach them" (9:3). Jesus' body was illuminated not by light shining from above but by light radiating from within, as he passed into a higher state of existence. It was at that moment, when God crowned Jesus with his glory, that the three disciples found themselves in a miraculous place between this world and the next.

God's power was also manifested after the death of Jesus. It was evident in Jesus' absence from the tomb where his body had been laid to rest. His might was manifested when, for forty days after his death, Jesus appeared to his disciples, telling them about the Kingdom of God. His power was apparent even to doubting Thomas who, being urged to place his finger in Jesus' side, said, "My Lord and my God!" (John 20:28). Finally, God's power was displayed in the Ascension, when Jesus "was taken up before their very eyes, and a cloud hid him from their sight. They were looking intently up into the sky as he was going, when suddenly two men dressed in white stood beside them. 'Men of Galilee,' they said, 'why do you stand here looking into the sky? This same Jesus, who has been taken from you into heaven, will come back in the same way you have seen him go into heaven'" (Acts 1:9-11). The awe his disciples must have felt standing in that place!

Jesus would rather have had people believe in him without having to see such miraculous sights. He lamented, "A wicked and adulterous generation asks for a miraculous sign!" (Matthew 12:39). He knew that miracles would not lead to lasting belief, as shown by the fickle faith of the people of the covenant time and time again. Some assert that miracles weaken faith in God because the faithful begin to depend more upon miracles than upon God, while the unfaithful see the miracle more than they see God. I, who consider myself one of the faithful, sometimes find this rationale for why God doesn't heal me a bitter pill to swallow. Especially since I have moments when I feel spiritually whole and healed— in Jesus—bathed in the radiance and peace of his presence in incredible places of thinness. If only those moments could last.

However, I must confess that I do wonder at times

whether my faith in God would wane if he did heal me
for good at those times. If the suffering that brought me
to seek him vanished, would I no longer feel the need to
seek him? The answer may lie in why Jesus appeals to
people like me in the first place.

Jesus sought out those who seemed to need him most
because they most needed to believe that life is more than
what it seems. That is why those who were detached from
life could most easily attach to Jesus and the idea of his
Kingdom. Sufferers such as me, who had come to the end
of themselves, could most easily find a beginning in him.
Why did Jesus teach that the world is tilted in favor of
the oppressed and the poor? It is because our only qualifi-
cation for God's grace is our emptiness and lack of
deservedness, which is also why we are most open to
receiving his grace.

I was sick. There was no doubt about it. I sought out
doctor after doctor until I finally received a definitive
diagnosis from a world-
famous researcher at the
Muscular Dystrophy Asso-
ciation. My illness also led
me to the Great Physician,
however, who by restoring
my faith in God healed
what ailed me most—even though he did not cure me. It
is the discrepancy between the two that has caused me
much angst.

Recently, I met with the dean of a seminary to discuss
the option of taking distance learning courses, since it is
difficult for me to attend a class on-site. When the dean
arrived, I was surprised to see that he was accompanied
by a pastor. Shortly into the interview, however, I realized

Jesus sought out those who seemed to need him most because they most needed to believe that life is more than what it seems.

the plan. The dean had brought her along to heal me—to anoint my head with oil in the name of Jesus Christ.

There we sat on my balcony, Pikes Peak looming in the distance, the Safeway parking lot across the street bustling with cars, as she made the sign of the cross on my forehead and began to pray fervently. I didn't know quite what to make of it. Part of me was grateful that she had come in Christ's love to try to cure me. Another part of me wondered whether this was some kind of admissions test. If I failed to heal, would the seminary reject me outright?

It's not that I don't believe in God's ability to heal us in various ways. It's just that, if God wants to heal me, I don't imagine it would necessarily take someone coming all the way from California to sit in the shadow of Safeway and anoint my head with oil. Nevertheless, I was open to the healing and prayed fervently right along with her. Unfortunately the healing didn't work. Nor did the seminary ever contact me. I choose to believe there is no connection between the two. Had the healing worked, however, I wonder whether I would be sitting here writing this book about Jesus—or golfing instead on the nearest straightaway, more in need of a caddy than a Creator. Would my desire to seek God's presence in thin places be eclipsed by the lure of attractions in this world?

I am convinced that the reason I am not healed is not because God doesn't love me. I know he does, because he came. Nor is it that he's indifferent, for he took on human limitations and pain. And it's certainly not because he's not powerful, because his power is manifested in miraculous ways. In all Jesus' actions, he demonstrated that God remains faithful to us. Is it possible that I just don't have enough faith in him?

It would seem a bit arrogant for me to assume that my chances for healing depend on the amount of my faith. I doubt I have such powers of influence over God. Rather, I believe that whether or not I am healed is not determined by my faith but by God's will. To argue that my faith is the determining factor in God's decisions is like saying that we are saved by works, not faith. How many good works would it take to be saved? How much faith would be enough to be healed? Would you need more faith to be healed of cancer than of a canker sore? Jesus did not issue a questionnaire to the blind and the lepers about the depth and consistency of their faith before he healed them. In fact, he healed anyone who asked. Jesus may not question my faith, although I sometimes do. However, I don't believe that my faith—or lack of it—is why he has not healed me.

Maybe my illness is a punishment—a life sentence without parole. First-century rabbis believed that the sick bring illness upon themselves because of sin. Jesus, however, did not accept this. Besides, it is inconceivable to me that the loving, caring, understanding God I know in Jesus would inflict such horrendous punishment upon his creation—especially not the God who died to set us free from sin and death. Jesus came to save humanity, not to condemn it. The good news Jesus preached was that he had come to redeem suffering and sin and to bring us to a far better place because he loves us.

One of Jesus' most beloved sits in front of me in her wheelchair on Sundays at church. She is five-and-a-half years old, has cerebellar hypoplasia and microcephaly. She has a seizure disorder, is fed through a g-tube, and is legally blind and deaf, although her parents believe—or at least hope—that she can see and hear something. She was born this way, and no one knows why. Her name is Haddie.

Every time I sit in my wheelchair behind Haddie in church, I feel as if I am in the presence of one of God's little angels, because her face glows with the love of Jesus Christ. There are times, however, when my face flushes in frustration as I witness one of the worst abominations on the face of the earth—a suffering child. Like Wiesel, I often look upward and point an accusing finger, asking *Why?*

Haddie's parents are loving, devoted, faithful Christians who keep the church body updated on Haddie's life. Several weeks ago, I received an e-mail from them that read, "Just a quick note to let you know that after Haddie broke her leg, she developed a huge pressure sore (ulcer) on her heel. After two long, hard weeks of her crying in pain with nothing to alleviate it, we knew something was not right. By the end of last week, it became infected and blistered and turned into what is called cellulitis. We were hoping to go to Young Life's family camp at Frontier Ranch on Friday, but Haddie was hospitalized due to the infection. . . . Please continue to pray for us. Her heel will take one to two months to heal. She also got a full leg cast today to better support her break. She was in a half cast that did not seem to provide enough support. We are hoping to send her to school sometime this week—pending that her foot is okay enough to go. She had to miss the first two days of kindergarten."

I have no idea why God allows Haddie to suffer so much. I am certain, however, that Jesus is in her. As Dr. Paul Brand, who was well acquainted with pain in his practice of medicine, said in response to the question,

Where is God when it hurts? "He is in *you*, the one hurt-
ing, not in *it*, the thing that hurts."[7]

If Jesus loves the sufferer so much that he is actually
in the one who suffers, why doesn't he heal little Haddie?
Why doesn't the master of miracles perform another one?
I don't know. What I do know is that when people look
at Haddie, they see not just a frail, suffering child but also
the power of Jesus within her, giving her strength and
encouraging those around her.

Paul knew as much as anyone that when we are weak,
we are strong. He wrote to the Corinthians, who valued
prestige and appearance, "If I must boast, I will boast of
the things that show my weakness. . . . Three times I
pleaded with the Lord to take it away from me. But he
said to me, 'My grace is sufficient for you, for my power
is made perfect in weakness.' Therefore I will boast all the
more gladly about my weaknesses, so that Christ's power
may rest on me" (2 Corinthians 11:30; 12:8-9). Paul
learned to rely on God when he could no longer rely on
himself. In the process, he discovered not only that he
was empowered by God but also that the divine power
within could have an amazing effect on others.

I have no doubt that Haddie—disabled, deaf, blind,
and wheelchair bound—causes others to see. But is that
fair? Why should Haddie have to suffer such misery? For
that matter, was the suffering and death of Jesus fair?
Maybe it was the only way God could show the contrast
between the immense unfairness of a fallen world and the
grace of his risen love. The death of Jesus in a fallen
world is ultimately the most important reason for his
coming—the cornerstone of Christianity. Jesus transforms
the meaning of suffering and death by suffering and
dying. As Peter Kreeft observes, "Vicarious atonement is

Christ's surprising solution to suffering. He destroys suffering by suffering!"⁸ On the cross, Jesus destroyed evil and transformed it into love. He paid the price for sin, so that death was no longer an ending but a beginning. He proved not through power but through love that there is no greater deed than to give your life for a friend. In sacrificial love, Jesus not only got us off the hook through substitutionary atonement but also got God off the hook by putting himself on the hook. Wiesel believed that God himself was hanged on the gallows of a concentration camp. I agree. God did hang on the gallows. But he did it to take our place. Wiesel could not forgive God for forsaking him. When Jesus felt forsaken by God and cried out, "My God, my God, why have you forsaken me?" (Matthew 27:46), he knew that being forsaken was the cost of God's forgiveness.

Yet incredibly, perched on that cross between earth and heaven, between this world and the next, Jesus did even more. He proved that just as he had transformed suffering and transcended death, we could do the same. We can be transformed in our trials and even transcend death if we go through them in him.

Reverend Peter Gomes, minister and professor at Harvard University, asserts, "The reason that the dying ask to see the cross before they die is to be reminded that Jesus has been where they now are, and that by his grace they are now to go where he is. Suffering, of which death is the ultimate expression, they know by the cross is a means, and not an end. They know that death was as real to Jesus as it is now to them. They know that he was not rescued in the nick of time. They know that when his hour was come he had to meet it, and that there was no way out; and they know also that that is true for them.

Knowing this, they also know that in the cross Jesus made it through and that he came out on the other side; their prayer is that what was promised and achieved in Jesus may be achieved for them as well."[9] Jesus, who is in us and with us, goes through our sufferings by our side—right to the other side.

Just as Jesus took the worst thing that could possibly happen and turned it into a victory, so can we. Some may try to deny pain, but Christians know that suffering exists as proof of our fallen state. Suffering is a fact of life, but it can be redeemed and transcended. Paul, after appealing to God to have a "thorn" in his side removed, prayed that his suffering would be redeemed, because he knew that Jesus could transform it. John Donne, bedridden and in despair, who first prayed that his suffering be removed, eventually offered prayers that it be redeemed. Joni Eareckson Tada, a quadriplegic who as a teenager broke her neck in a diving accident and has been confined to a wheelchair for years, claims her accident was the best thing that ever happened to her because it turned her toward God. Amazingly, God not only got her attention but the attention of others who see his work displayed in her life. But is that enough? Does that justify such horrible suffering?

Jesus destroyed evil and transformed it into love. He paid the price for sin, so that death was no longer an ending but a beginning.

Joni once said of her life, "It's a daily, hard-fought-for, desperate pulling down of grace from heaven."[10] What can someone who suffers relentlessly possibly mean by grace? If I were to define God's grace as his giving me everything I want, I would conclude that he is not a very gracious God. After all, he has not restored what I have lost. I continue to suffer from a disabling illness, and I live alone on a very limited income. Well-meaning Christians, in an attempt to encourage me have said, "God doesn't give us everything we want, but he gives us everything we need." I have always wanted to ask them what their definition of *need* is. Do I need to be able to walk, get out of bed, feed myself? Does Haddie need to be able to see and hear, run and play with other children? Living in my body, in a physical world, just how much of what I want is, indeed, what I need? I don't know—which may not be a bad thing. That's because the answer is not what I need, but what God needs of me. It's not an answer I always feel good about. It's just the way it is.

As I see it, God balances needs. His system may not seem to favor each of us all the time, but it ultimately favors all of us. We cannot know the Lord's eternal plan. He made that quite clear to Job when he said, "Where were you when I laid the earth's foundation? Tell me, if you understand" (Job 38:4). We may not understand, but we can trust that God, in his infinite wisdom, works all things for the good.

Joni's ministry is proof that if we trust in Jesus, God will work in us for the good. As it says in Romans, "Suffering produces perseverance; perseverance, character; and character, hope" (5:3-4). Despite quadriplegia, or maybe because of it, Joni has given hope to millions as a renowned speaker, radio host, acclaimed writer, artist, and singer. She also funds the distribution of wheelchairs to the poor in nations around the world. Whenever I hear Joni speak, I hear the grace of God in her voice, reminding me of the inspired words of Paul, who wrote that God's grace was sufficient for him.

When I first became a believer, I read those words but

couldn't understand what Paul meant. In my life, God's grace was necessary but certainly not sufficient for me. It was only when I began to walk with Jesus that I truly understood.

Those who are acquainted with my life wonder how I manage to survive day by day. The pain in my muscles is often intense. I am constantly fatigued and sometimes too weak to rise from bed. I have poor digestion, which makes eating difficult. I have too slow a heartbeat and too high a temperature. I have neurological episodes that land me on the floor and, when I am upright, cause me to shake so badly that I can hardly feed myself. Yesterday I was trying to eat turkey when a friend of mine called. My hands and arms were so tremulous that the fork was literally shaking as it entered my mouth. I jokingly remarked, "This turkey hasn't moved so fast since the day it was killed."

I could go on with a litany of my symptoms, but suffice it to say that mitochondrial encephalomyopathy—one of the over forty neuromuscular diseases being researched by the Muscular Dystrophy Association—affects the mitochondria (energy factories present in almost every cell of the body). My mitochondria are severely deficient in vital chemicals necessary to produce ATP, which powers the cells of the body. Enough said. Yet if my mother were alive, I know that she would be astonished at how much hope I have, even though my illness continues to worsen.

That's because while my days are difficult and God doesn't seem to be healing me at the moment, his grace is manifested everywhere I look and has been since the moment I met Jesus. God's grace has meant leading me to a loving church, where I gave my testimony when I first became a Christian. In the congregation was a copy edi-

tor who offered to help me write my first book when I
didn't have the money to pay for assistance. By grace, the
book was published, even though I was an unknown
author lying in a sickbed. That book has enabled me to
reach thousands of readers with my story for God's glory.
It was grace that the literary agent who found a publisher
for my book became a cherished friend. And grace that
she drove me all the way from Boston to my new home in
Colorado because flying is difficult for me. Whenever I
stare into the loving eyes of such amazing friends, I see
Jesus lovingly gazing back at me. That is grace. It is by
grace that this failing body finds the strength to pen these
words. And grace when God is palpably present, giving
me inspiration—and really good edits. It is also grace
when, in the darkest nights, exhausted and in pain from
writing, I whisper the name of Jesus, and he comes to
comfort me as he did the first moment I came to know
him. It is all by his amazing grace.

By grace, God breaks into my suffering daily in places
that bear the mark of his mighty and loving hand. Just as
he handily broke through the veil, coming into this world
in amazing places such as Mount Sinai, in Jesus himself,
and finally in the Holy Spirit, who fills us with his presence. For on the day of Pentecost, when the disciples were
all together in one place, "suddenly a sound like the
blowing of a violent wind came from heaven and filled
the whole house where they were sitting. They saw what
seemed to be tongues of fire that separated and came to
rest on each of them. All of them were filled with the
Holy Spirit and began to speak in other tongues as the
Spirit enabled them" (Acts 2:2-4).

Jesus will come again. Until that day, the Spirit lives
on in us, passing through the frontier into our hearts,

more real than the body, more real than death itself. We do not suffer without hope nor do we go it alone, because Jesus gave us the Spirit, who "helps us in our weakness . . . intercedes for us with groans that words cannot express" (Romans 8:26). In fact, the Spirit is a deposit on the life to come.

What is the answer to suffering? The answer is who Jesus is. Jesus is not only the embodiment of God himself. He is also the embodiment of God's love and grace.

When Jesus became the crossroads between this world and the next, everything changed forever. In that miraculous moment in history, God—in Jesus—showed us he loves us by coming to earth. He showed us he cares by becoming one of us. He showed us he understands by sharing in our suffering. He showed us his hope for us by dying on a cross to redeem our sins and assure us of eternity. God gave us all this by the grace of Jesus, in miraculous places of thinness.

> When Jesus became the crossroads between this world and the next, everything changed forever.

God is still behind the veil, waiting for us in heaven. But because of Jesus—the ultimate thin place—we can recognize God's face and can see his hand in our lives in thin places all around us.

Such grace is sufficient for me.

Chapter 7

What Am I? Dust Falling, Spirit Rising

We are not only made of earth. We are also made of heaven.

By grace, I can see Jesus' hand in my life. Yet I must confess that there are moments when I want even more. I long to feel his literal touch. How preposterous, some would say! How can we, who have been born long after Jesus walked the earth, possibly feel the touch of God? The answer is, we can because we already have. It's because of *what* we're made of.

You needn't search your memory for the miraculous moment when God's touch was first upon you. It's a primal experience so deep, so miraculous, that it can barely be comprehended, let alone consciously remembered. Our inability to remember the moment doesn't mean it never happened, however. We are living proof that it did. Each of us carries an indelible imprint from the hand of God because his was the hand that made us. Somewhere deep within us is a memory of a loving, divine caress that gently brushed our soul at the very moment of creation, leaving us yearning for more.

Why is it so difficult for us to feel God's touch in our lives? Why do we sometimes feel as if we know everything about Jesus, but don't really know him? Why doesn't he seem real enough, immediate enough? A practicing Christian recently said to me, "The problem is, I feel like I know too much but feel too little. I believe in Jesus, but I can't seem to sense his presence." These concerns have plagued Christians who have looked to God for answers throughout the ages. Yet the answer may have less to do with God than with ourselves.

Each of us carries an indelible imprint from the hand of God because his was the hand that made us.

Recently my good friend Alice invited me to speak in front of her church's singles' group, which meets on Friday evenings. I was hesitant to accept her invitation because by that time of night, I am usually so worn out that episodes of shaking and stuttering are common. What would happen if I had an episode during my speech? I worried. Nevertheless, I accepted the invitation and prayed for the best, not wanting to let a good friend down.

On the evening of my speech, I sat next to Alice, singing praise-and-worship music before being called up to speak. As the hour grew later and later, I felt myself growing more tired by the minute. I tried to distract myself by swaying gently in rhythm to the music.

All of a sudden, parts of me started swaying on their own. First my right leg shook, then my right arm. Then my left arm joined in. By the time I leaned over to Alice to whisper, "I'm starting to have an episode," it was a full-blown attack. To make matters worse, stuttering soon followed. "Do you want to skip the speech?" Alice inquired in a worried tone. "No," I said resolutely, with a couple of extra *n*'s. What I couldn't tell her—even if I could have formed the words—was that I had no earthly idea how I was going to make it up to the stage, let alone deliver a speech.

Alice gently put her hand on my knee to try to stop the shaking and closed her eyes to pray for me. Tense moments passed, but nothing changed. Despite the lofty music and fervent prayer, it seemed that God had not even bothered to show up.

Martin Buber, a Jewish theologian and philosopher, once noted, "The Bible knows of God's hiding His face, of times when the contact between Heaven and earth seems to be interrupted. God seems to withdraw Himself utterly from the earth and no longer to participate in its existence. The space of history is then full of noise, but as it were, empty of divine breath."[1] I held my breath as I strained to feel God's, but I could not sense even a wisp. Fearing the worst, I believed I would have to either abandon the talk to save face or attempt to make it up to the podium, red faced, horribly embarrassed by my spastic body and halting speech.

I began to chastise myself. *Don't I know better than to rely on my body at this time of night? I'll bet the moment I attempt to rise from this chair, I'll fall flat on my face right to the ground. How fitting. Dust to dust.* The furthest thing from my mind that night was on whom I really should have been relying—and of what else he had made me.

The Bible tells us that we are indeed made from the dust of the earth. Yet it also tells us that we are so much more. For when the Lord gave us life, he breathed into us his life-giving spirit. As it says in Genesis, "So God created man in his own image, in the image of God he created him; male and female he created them" (Genesis 1:27). Why would a transcendent and omnipotent God breathe his very own spirit into a creature made of dust?

Elihu had one answer for this puzzling question when he said to Job, "It is the spirit in a man, the breath of the Almighty, that gives him understanding. It is not only the old who are wise, not only the aged who understand what is right" (Job 32:8-9). Paul tells us, "The man without the Spirit does not accept the things that come from the Spirit of God, for they are foolishness to him, and he cannot understand them, because they are spiritually discerned" (1 Corinthians 2:14). It is clear that, by endowing us with his Spirit, God gave us a capacity for spiritual understanding. What is even more amazing is that because God's Spirit is within us, we can achieve communion—and even union—with him, spirit to Spirit. As Thomas Merton, Trappist monk and prolific spiritual writer, observed, "Since our souls are spiritual substances and since God is pure Spirit, there is nothing to prevent a union between ourselves and Him that is ecstatic in the literal sense of the word."[2]

Unfortunately it wasn't the Spirit moving me that night as I sat shaking and stuttering uncontrollably, waiting to go onstage. In fact, I could feel no connection with the Spirit at all. That was surprising, since if anyone is convinced of the reality of the Spirit, it's me. In fact, I once thought I literally felt the Spirit rise from a body far worse off than mine—way before I became a Christian.

It was a chilly morning in April when I was awakened from a fitful sleep in the predawn hours by my frantic father. He had just received the dreaded call from the ICU that my mother, who had lapsed into a coma ten days after open-heart surgery, had only hours to live. My first thought at the time was to turn over and resume sleeping. I didn't see much good in involving myself in the inevitable. Would it really make a difference whether I was there to witness my mother's last breath? I wondered. My comatose mother probably would not know the difference anyway. Nor would the incomprehensible, seemingly uninvolved God who was letting her die. Those were my rationalizations. But the real reason was that I was afraid to watch her die—again.

As a child, I would sometimes awaken in the dark crying after dreaming about her death. My mother would always come to my bedside to comfort and reassure me with her well-worn adage: "My mother used to say, if you dream about a person's death, it won't happen." Unfortunately I was not dreaming about my mother's death the day I was summoned to her bedside to watch her die.

By the time my father and I arrived at the hospital, my brother was already there, chanting the Shema, the holiest prayer in Judaism, over my mother's dying body. "Hear, O Israel: The Lord our God, the Lord is one" (Deuteronomy 6:4), he repeated over and over in such plaintive cries that even the atheist in the next bed was beginning to believe. The atheist in our family was not, however. My father was so beside himself that he could not bring himself to sit beside his wife, let alone pray. He stood at the foot of the bed, frozen in fear, while I stationed myself opposite my brother. Not knowing what to do, I took my mother's hand and began whispering last words to her, interspersing "I love you" as many times as I could. I even chanted the Shema several times, just in case God really was present and would appreciate the effort. Besides, I knew that my prayers would please my mother—that is, if she could hear them through the thick fog of the coma that was slowly claiming her body. Meanwhile, I watched the numbers on the monitor sink gravely. It would be only a matter of minutes before we would switch from chanting the Shema to saying the Kaddish, the mourner's prayer for the dead. Yet not before we found ourselves in a very thin place between places, straddling between earth and heaven.

Just before my mother took her last breath, my brother and I did something we cannot explain, even to this day. Simultaneously we placed our hands on her body. Suddenly something amazing happened. At first, I wasn't sure it had happened at all, until my brother asked, "Did you feel that?" As my eyes met his, I tried to speak but stood dumbfounded, afraid to acknowledge what I thought he meant. Finally, in a hushed tone, I murmured "I think I did. I think I felt something go right through my—" My brother cut me off, words rushing out of his mouth before he could catch them. "Something rose through my hands too!" he exclaimed. I found myself wondering whether my mother was staring down upon us both, hoping we would believe in what we could not see.

In that end-of-life coma, in the twilight between life and death, had my mother come to know the Truth? I will never know, although to this day I long to find out. I am convinced, however, that standing on the border between life and death, heaven and earth, as my mother took her last breath, what we observed was not dust falling but spirit rising, affirming that when God breathed into our lifeless bodies of clay, he gifted each of us with a soul. As it says in Matthew, "Do not be afraid of those who kill the body but cannot kill the soul" (10:28). While the body returns to dust, the regenerate soul turns toward heaven, rising victoriously from the earth.

So if we are spirit and God is Spirit, why couldn't I feel his healing touch upon me the night of my speech? What was getting in the way? The answer has something to do with what happened a very long time ago—in the Garden of Eden.

It was a miraculous moment for humanity when God created Paradise for Adam and Eve and pronounced it good. Adam and Eve were not so certain, however. Led to believe by the serpent that God was holding out on them and there was even greater good to be had, the first couple became dissatisfied. Motivated by the prospect of gaining divinity, they violated God's trust by eating the forbidden fruit. According to Genesis, "When the woman saw that the fruit of the tree was good for food and pleasing to the eye, and also desirable for gaining wisdom, she took some and ate it. She also gave some to her husband, who was with her, and he ate it. Then the eyes of both of them were opened, and they realized they were naked; so they sewed fig leaves together and made coverings for themselves" (3:6-7). As Allen Ross, biblical scholar and author of *Creation and Blessing*, notes, "The results, of course, were anticlimactic. Their eyes (i.e., their understanding) were opened, but the promise of divine enlightenment did not come about. What was right before was now very wrong. They knew more, but that additional knowledge was evil. They saw more, but what they

When God breathed into our lifeless bodies of clay, he gifted each of us with a soul.

now saw they spoiled by seeing. Mistrust and alienation replaced the security and intimacy they had enjoyed."[3] Sadly, the harmonious relationship Adam and Eve had once shared with the Lord was broken, leading to conflict and alienation. To hide their shame, Adam and Eve covered themselves with fig leaves, while taking cover behind the trees in the Garden to shield themselves from God's wrath. Yet in disobeying God, Adam and Eve had put far more between God and themselves than mere fig leaves and trees. They had allowed their selfish egos, riddled with guilt, to come between them and their Creator, forever thickening the veil.

Life would never be the same as God created it. Jesus would come to die for our sins, reestablishing our access to God. He would inaugurate his Kingdom which, when fully realized, will banish evil and restore God's reign over all the earth. Until that time, however, we live in between times, in a kingdom both "now" and "not yet," still sullied by the consequences of the Fall.

It would have been wonderful if the coming of Jesus to earth had restored our relationship with the Lord to one of complete harmony. It didn't, because we remain fallen creatures in relationship with a perfect God. As Philip Yancey observes, "When we receive God's grace and spiritual life begins, tension increases as well. A perfect saint would experience no tension, nor would a sinner untroubled by guilt. The rest of us must live somewhere between the two extremes, which complicates rather than simplifies life."[4] Our dual nature causes the tension within ourselves and ultimately between us

> We live in between times, in a kingdom both "now" and "not yet," still sullied by the consequences of the Fall.

and our Creator. As fallen creatures, we fall victim to our propensity to sin even while striving to do good. Evelyn Underhill, prolific British writer on spiritual growth, observes, "We are creatures of sense and spirit, and we must live an amphibious life."[5] It is not easy to live an amphibious life when you have clay feet.

If the story of the Garden of Eden seems remote, if not irrelevant, consider how we use our free will today. We may yearn for God's presence, but how many of us, like Adam and Eve, let our own egos get in the way? I must confess that, as I sat waiting to go onto the stage that night, clay feet shaking, all I could think about was myself. What kind of faithful follower was I?

Maybe I'm being too hard on myself. After all, there is nothing more difficult than for a mere mortal of flesh and blood to trust an invisible God, even if he is within us. Not only can we not see him but we also are not privy to the overall picture. We are given only a small piece of the puzzle, while he knows the grand design. We are destined to live life forward but can only understand it backward. It's no wonder that in the dead of night we most acutely feel the pain of groping in the dark. Yet Philip Yancey tells us, "I never 'see' God. I seldom run into visual clues that remind me of God unless I am looking. The act of looking, the pursuit itself, makes possible the encounter. For this reason, Christianity has always insisted that trust and obedience come first, and knowledge follows."[6] Is it possible that when it comes to a personal relationship with an invisible God all we can do is trust first—and then wait?

My waiting ended when I was finally called to speak and labored to make my way up the two steps leading to the stage. My body was weak and in a great deal of pain, so someone graciously brought a chair onstage for me. I eyed the seat gratefully, craving the comfort it would provide. But in the split second it would have taken to plant myself down, I found myself forcing my body up to the podium. Leaning heavily on my crutches for support, I said in a weak voice, "It's way past my bedtime, and I should be in bed by now." The crowd, mostly in their forties and fifties, laughed. The last time any of them had gone to bed at nine o'clock was probably when they were ten. As I strained to remain erect, my legs began to sag more and more. Securing my grip on my crutches, I pressed on, "In fact, not only should I not be up now, but I also shouldn't even be sitting up in that chair." I paused for several long seconds to catch my breath. "So I've decided to stand." The surprised audience burst into applause, yet no one was more surprised than I. Since being stricken with this disease, I had not been able to stand, crutches or no crutches, for more than a few minutes at a time—and the speech I was about to give was scheduled to last at least twenty-five minutes. I could feel my mind conspiring to dissuade me from such a foolish idea, while my heart remained undaunted. Gathering courage, I proclaimed, "Either you trust the promises of Jesus or you don't. There is no middle ground. And if you don't trust his promises, then you really don't know him."

In the midst of the renewed applause, something truly amazing happened. Suddenly I was bathed in a yellow-white light. My buckling knees straightened, the muscles in my arms clutching the crutches strengthened, and all my pain vanished. I felt a flow of energy race through every cell of my body. In the thin place that materialized in front of my very eyes and enveloped my body, I found myself no longer standing under my own power—but because of his. I could almost hear Jesus whisper to me, "Since you are willing to stand up for me, I will stand for you." It was one of the most extraordinary moments of my life.

Yet it was a quite ordinary moment for our Lord. Doesn't he often reward our faith and service with even greater blessings for us? Why should I have been surprised that when I struggled to stand for him, he would stand for me?

I scrapped most of my notes that night to speak as the Lord led me. "You know, I am healed in moments, and this is one of those moments. I don't know how long it will last this time. It could last forever or not until I get off this stage. Yet what I do know for a fact is that in this moment I am healed." Alice later told me that everyone in the room gasped.

That night I stood there for the full twenty-five minutes, well past 9 p.m., delivering my speech with energy and no pain. I even took questions from the audience. Then, as I turned to leave the stage, I once *I am healed in moments, and this is one of those moments.* again felt the heavy weight of my legs as weakness overtook my body and pain returned to my muscles. In the midst of the standing ovation that erupted, I was struggling to stand. Alice immediately came to my rescue, helping me down the steps. "That was awesome!" she whispered in my ear.

She was not alone in her amazement. Those who were there that night believed that they had witnessed a rare miracle. I know otherwise. For in the darkest of nights, when I lie in bed shaking and in pain, I often call upon

Jesus, and he comes to me in healing moments, giving my body peace and rest. Why had I doubted he would do that again that night? Was it because those healing moments don't always happen when I wish they would? Sadly, sometimes the hardest thing for me to do is to get out of my own way and trust in his.

Paul was obedient and trusted God, regardless of circumstances. He wrote, "I have learned the secret of being content in any and every situation, whether well fed or hungry, whether living in plenty or in want" (Philippians 4:12). Jeremiah knew well the blessings of trust, saying:

Sometimes the hardest thing for me to do is to get out of my own way and trust in his.

"Blessed is the man who trusts in the Lord, whose confidence is in him. He will be like a tree planted by the water that sends out its roots by the stream. It does not fear when heat comes; its leaves are always green. It has no worries in a year of drought and never fails to bear fruit" (Jeremiah 17:7-8). In the book of Hebrews, where faith is defined as "being sure of what we hope for and certain of what we do not see" (11:1), there is a list of many of our forebears who lived not by sight but by faith—obedient believers such as Noah, who built an ark before it rained; Abraham, who was prepared to offer his only son as a sacrifice; Moses, who led his people through the Red Sea. These faithful servants trusted first and then obeyed.

Yet how many of us are spiritual giants? Even after experiencing many healing moments with God in the past, I had not trusted he would do it again that night. "Surely the Lord is in this place, and I was not aware of it," Jacob declared (Genesis 28:16). The good news is that even when we fail to be faithful and trust in God, God remains faithful to us. Like a good parent, he accepts us regardless of our faults. Despite our betrayals, he remains loyal. The Lord even gave Peter the responsibility of building his church, even though Peter had denied Jesus three times. Over and over again, Jesus showed his willingness to be faithful, even to the less than faithful. He waits for us to return to him in faith, as he did for the disciples: "Do not let your hearts be troubled. Trust in God; trust also in me" (John 14:1).

I asked God to place his healing touch upon me that night. But as Alice sat fervently praying for me, I was more concerned about being embarrassed onstage or forfeiting my speech than faithfully serving the Lord. How can I ask God to put his trust in me, if I don't place my trust in him? How can I ask him to be there for me, if I'm not willing to be there for him? I want God to be passionate about me, but how consistently passionate am I about him? I ask him to understand me, but how hard do I try to understand him? I desire that he spend time with me, but how much time am I willing to spend with him? I want him to listen to me, but do I always listen to him? I ask him to give me even more than what he has already sacrificed for me, but how much am I willing to sacrifice for him? I want his commitment to me, but do I remain truly committed to him? I want God to share a personal relationship with me, but how willing am I to get personal with him?

Why is it so hard to experience God's loving touch? Maybe God observes the same thing about us when he reaches out to touch us and doesn't feel the warm glow of an ethereal spirit but rather the rough edges of a clay pot.

We become hardened to God whenever we become

full of ourselves—when we forget we are God breathed and fall victim to the tension between the earthly and spiritual parts of ourselves—sinning instead of soaring above our circumstances in him. The veil thickens every time we allow our egos to come between us and God— every time we mistrust him, think he is holding out on us, believe we know better than he does, doubt he will work all things for the good, and ask more of him than we do of ourselves.

The good news is that the Spirit within us works to transform us for the good. For we are not only made of earth. We are also made of heaven. It is because of *what* we are—not merely dust falling but also spirit rising— that we can be "touched by Him Who has no hands, but Who is pure Reality and the source of all that is real!" as Thomas Merton wrote.[7] For by grace we can feel the warmth of God's loving embrace.

Chapter 8

Why Am I? Made for Spiritual Embrace

We are not only made for relationship with each other. We are also made for relationship with God.

It is nothing short of amazing that we can feel God's touch upon us. Yet many of us crave even more. We yearn to be able to make such encounters happen predictably. How absurd, you may say. In the first place, how do you know that at any one moment God wants to encounter you? The answer may lie in *why* we are here in the first place.

When I was young, my parents often hosted Sunday barbecues. My mother and my aunt Sophie would make potato salad and coleslaw from scratch. Uncle Irv would take refuge in the hammock, while my father would take on the daunting task of lighting the barbecue.

Dad was not a whiz at such things, although he had developed an admirable routine. He would emerge from the garage toting a portable grill, a large bag of Kingsford charcoal, a can of lighter fluid, and his tattered work gloves. All ingredients present and accounted for, he would carefully put on his gloves like a surgeon, meticulously arrange the coals in a symmetrical mound, and liberally sprinkle lighter fluid on the pile. Pulling a special box of wooden matches out of his pocket, he would strike the flint and toss the lighted match onto the coals. Then he would wait for a big burst of flames—which usually never happened. Out came the can of lighter fluid again. More drenching of the coals, a lit match flicked onto the pile—then nothing. "How's the fire going, Mac?" my mother would yell from the kitchen. "Fine," my father would yell back, grabbing the can of lighter fluid again, shaking it more vigorously this time. I would watch the scene with conflicting emotions. While I couldn't wait for the sight of hot, juicy burgers crackling on the grill, I worried that if the lighter fluid–drenched coals ever did ignite, the explosion would blow up the whole neighborhood.

Every Sunday Dad would repeat the same ritual, and occasionally the coals would actually catch fire on the first try. He never could figure out why sometimes the coals ignited immediately and at other times they didn't.

My spiritual life is a lot like Sunday barbecues. Sometimes a divine spark ignites my heart, and at other times it doesn't. This has caused me to wonder, *What can I do to ensure an encounter with God?* If the Lord is always with us, what's the problem? The answer goes back to Old Testament times.

In the lives of the early Hebrews, God made spectacular appearances that by today's standards would seem hard to miss. After all, how difficult is it to hook up with a deity who shows up in bolts of lightning and blasts of thunder, as God did on Mount Sinai? Yet soon after the Lord withdrew from the mountain, the Israelites were busy fashioning a golden calf to worship: "Come, make us gods who will go before us. As for this fellow Moses who brought us up out of Egypt, we don't know what has happened to him" (Exodus 32:1). Moses had only been gone a few weeks, yet the Israelites already assumed they had been forsaken. Or were they never quite convinced in the first place of what they had seen?

I've often wondered how the Israelites would have responded to an exit poll after God came and went from Mount Sinai. Would they have said that they believed without a doubt that what they saw was a manifestation of God? How many would wonder if maybe they had had too much to drink the night before? Would some think they were going a little crazy? Or would others believe that what they had experienced was part of a mass hallucination?

This may sound far fetched, until we fast-forward to another amazing period in history when God appeared again—this time in the person of Jesus Christ. John wrote poignantly of Jesus' arrival, "He was in the world, and though the world was made through him, the world did not recognize him. He came to that which was his own, but his own did not receive him" (1:10-11). When Jesus, God incarnate, appeared on earth, one would think that God's presence would have been unmistakable. It's not as if Jesus hid who he was. Yet when the Lord was brought before the chief priests and teachers of the law and was asked, "If you are the Christ . . . tell us," Jesus answered, "If I tell you, you will not believe me" (Luke 22:67). Why didn't Jesus take the opportunity to declare his identity in front of such a distinguished court? Was it because Jesus knew that the Pharisees had hardened their hearts and nothing he could say or do would have convinced them of his divinity?

Even one of Jesus' own disciples doubted. Thomas demanded, "Unless I see the nail marks in his hands and put my finger where the nails were, and put my hand into his side, I will not believe it" (John 20:25). Only when Jesus invited doubting Thomas to place his fingers into the nail holes in Jesus' risen body did the humbled disciple exclaim, "My Lord and my God!" (verse 28). Jesus replied, "Because you have seen me, you have believed; blessed are those who have not seen and yet have believed" (verse 29).

If the apostle Thomas, encountering the risen Christ, still needed physical proof to believe, how much hope is there for the rest of us who struggle to discern the presence of an invisible God? How much harder is it for us to detect the more subtle yet equally extraordinary movements God makes every day in the ordinary moments of our lives?

"When he passes me, I cannot see him; when he goes by, I cannot perceive him," lamented Job (9:11). We, like Job, can be blind to the stirrings of an invisible God. We long to develop eyes to see and ears to hear, but how? A time-honored tradition is the practice of spiritual disciplines. Unfortunately this may not be the answer you want to hear. Initially neither did I.

When I became a Christian, I thought my life would be a series of multiple epiphanies, patterned on the moment when I first met Jesus. My mother had always taught me that Christians were far happier than Jews. "They have more to be happy about," she would say, with a tinge of envy in her voice. "They are contented cows." I never understood what livestock had to do with Christianity—outside of the crèche, that is—but I dared not ask. My mother had already told me more than she knew.

It wasn't until I converted to Christianity that I realized that Christians are not happy all the time—especially me. Nor was I thrilled to discover that just when I thought I had finally escaped the rituals and requirements of Jewish law, I was supposed to practice spiritual disciplines, which would somehow lead to joy. A friend once remarked to me, "Who has the time to practice spiritual gymnastics? I can hardly manage as it is, with my job, my kids, and working out at the gym three times a week. You should see my house. It's a mess." Another told me in frustration, "I've tried spiritual disciplines, and they don't work. Besides, after a while they become more of a burden than a help." Imagine my surprise when I discovered that the disciplines were not meant to burden us but to free us.

This really shouldn't have surprised me. In Judaism, the law may *seem* restrictive, but it was never meant to restrict freedom. Instead the law was designed to create freedom by allowing the observant Jew to say no to appetite. The Torah (the first five books of the Old Testament), which contains 613 commandments, provides a framework to accomplish this goal. Although few Jews actually obey all these commandments, they still regard the Torah as the essence of Jewish spirituality, because the sacred scroll contains the very foundations of Jewish wisdom, learning, and love of God. As Rabbi Morris Kertzer so eloquently comments, "To the observant Jew, the Torah is the very breath of life."[1]

Jewish laws and rituals are not only meant to control human appetites, however, but also to sanctify them. For

I discovered that the disciplines were not meant to burden us but to free us.

example, by keeping kosher, Jews sanctify the act of eating. By giving charity, they sanctify the desire to amass material goods. By adhering to law and performing rituals, thus honoring God, the ordinary is made holy. This is not to say that Jews are called to live an ascetic life. Judaism not only discourages excess but also asceticism. God's bounty is supposed to be enjoyed in moderation.

It is interesting to note that when Christians look upon Jewish practices and observances, they often see the restriction more than the freedom. Likewise, when Jews observe Christians practicing the disciplines, they often say the same. Yet according to Richard Foster, an acclaimed writer on Christian spirituality, "The purpose of the Disciplines is freedom. Our aim is the freedom, not the Discipline. The moment we make the Discipline our central focus, we turn it into law and lose the corresponding freedom."[2] He observes, "God has ordained the Disciplines of the spiritual life as the means by which we place ourselves where he can bless us."[3] Just as Jewish believers consider themselves blessed when, in adhering to God's law, they draw closer to him, Christians who practice the disciplines find themselves graced when they achieve a deeper relationship with Jesus.

The disciplines grace us with a deeper relationship with Jesus.

What are the spiritual disciplines, and how do they bless us? The disciplines include prayer, silence, solitude, meditation, and fasting, among others. One way they bless us is by freeing us from internal and external distractions so that we may experience God's still, small voice within.

When I began practicing the disciplines, I was disappointed to find that my experiences of God's presence were inconsistent. What was I doing wrong? I wondered. Why couldn't I encounter God whenever I called upon him? I finally discovered that it had less to do with God being there than with *why* I am here.

It all began when I fell victim to a virus that relegated me to bed with symptoms of nausea, fever, chills, sweats, and pain. To make matters worse, all the usual symptoms of my neuromuscular disease were intensified. I lay in a pool of sweat, moaning—and bemoaning my fate.

I tried to bring myself to pray but couldn't. When a friend called, I jokingly remarked, "I would pray for you, but I'm not talking to Jesus right now." It was no laughing matter, however. In fact, after I hung up the phone, I felt guilty about what I had said.

Yet everyone has periods of spiritual dryness. Spiritual notables tell us to pray anyway, whether we feel spiritually dry or not, because God appreciates our efforts.

As I lay in bed struggling hard to pray, I was haunted by all the times I had prayed—in vain—for healing. Why hadn't God responded to my pleas for a cure? I wondered. "Only God knows," I muttered in frustration.

What I did know, however, was that I was not alone. The psalmist lamented, "O my God, I cry out by day, but you do not answer" (Psalm 22:2). Jesus himself cried out from the cross, "My God, my God, why have you forsaken me?" (Matthew 27:46). C. S. Lewis asserted, "Every war, every famine or plague, almost every death-bed, is the monument to a petition that was not granted."[4] As I struggled to pray, I wondered if my prayers for healing hadn't been granted because I hadn't prayed well enough. Was there was a special prayer formula known only by a blessed few? Patron saint Jeanne de Chantal didn't believe so. She echoed the sentiments of many fellow prayer journeyers when she stated, "The great method of prayer is to have no method at all. Prayer happens by grace, not by artfulness."[5] Jesus taught us to say the Lord's Prayer, but he didn't limit us to scripted prayer. Nor did he confine himself to prayer rituals. In fact, he lived a life of prayer, being prayerful in everything he said and did. One might say that he himself was a living prayer. Yet even Jesus seemed to suffer unanswered prayer.

Think positively, I told myself as I turned over in bed, searching for a less painful position. Maybe I shouldn't focus on what the illness is doing to me but rather on what it has done *for* me. After all, if I had never fallen ill, I would never have been able to rise in Jesus. My illness has not only led me to God but has also fostered a continuing and profound attachment to him. In appealing to God day after day for strength, my relationship with him has strengthened. In petitioning him to heal me, my humility has grown. I may become silent in frustration and even angry at times when my requests appeared to be denied, but I remain anything but indifferent. Like a disenchanted lover, my anger connects me even more to him, the strength of my rage proportionate to the amount of my love. Elie Wiesel may have wanted anything but an indifferent God. But God, who is anything but indifferent, wants anything but our indifference.

Lying in that bed, I recalled how Jesus had redeemed my suffering for the good. I felt so encouraged that I offered up a prayer of thanks, one for healing, and a request that he make his presence known to me. Then I lay back on my pillow, waiting for a response. Nothing happened. My frustration returned.

"Didn't Jesus promise to give us what we ask?" I muttered to myself. He tells us in the Bible, "Ask and it will be given to you; seek and you will find; knock and the door will be opened to you. For everyone who asks receives; he who seeks finds; and to him who knocks, the door will be opened" (Matthew 7:7-8). So why hasn't he answered me? Or has he answered by saying no? P. T. Forsyth, a twentieth-century theologian, believed, "We shall come one day to a heaven where we shall gratefully know that God's great refusals were sometimes the true answers to our truest prayer."[6] Yet with my fever rising and my muscles screaming in pain, I couldn't rest in that answer.

A wave of nausea came over me, and I heaved into a basin. "At least I'm emptying myself," I quipped to no one listening. But have I emptied myself enough spiritually to let God in? I prayed to the Lord again, this time asking him to grant me the strength to empty myself so that he could fill me with his presence.

The Brief Rule of Saint Romuald (952–1027) instructs, "Empty yourself completely and sit waiting, content with the grace of God, like the chick who tastes nothing and eats nothing but what his mother brings to him."[7] God only fills empty hands, so we must empty ourselves, particularly of the sins of self that separate us from him. According to A. W. Tozer, known for his loving and relentless pursuit of God, those sins are "self-righteousness, self-pity, self-confidence, self-sufficiency, self-admiration, self-love and a host of others like them. . . . Self is the opaque veil that hides the face of God from us."[8]

I lay in bed trying hard to empty myself as much as I could. Meanwhile, I continued stumbling through more words of prayer. Suddenly I realized something. How can I empty myself while my mouth remains full of words? I chastised myself and then fell silent so that I could hear God's voice within.

"Be still, and know that I am God," quoted the psalmist (Psalm 46:10). Francois Fénelon, a seventeenth-century scholar and educator, instructed, "Be silent, and listen to God. Let your heart be in such a state of preparation that his Spirit may impress upon you such virtues as will please him. Let all within you listen to him. This silence of all outward and earthly affection and of human thoughts within us is essential if we are to hear his voice."[9] We become silent not merely to refrain from speech but to detach from earthly preoccupations and to meditate upon what is essential: the living God. We do not remain detached from life, however, but reenter our lives with new insight and perspective, having made a place in our hearts for God to abide.

In silence I meditated on God until another wave of nausea rudely interrupted me. I decided to force myself from bed in search of a dry cracker. Grabbing my walker, I slowly headed for the kitchen, while meditating along the way.

We can be engaged in the world and still meditate, ordering our mental life on many different levels at once. That's what Brother Lawrence, a lay brother at the monastery of the Discalced Carmelites in the seventeenth century, described us. He was a pious man who strove to meditate on the things of God every waking hour, living his life in accordance with Paul's advice in Thessalonians: "Pray continually; give thanks in all circumstances, for this is God's will for you in Christ Jesus" (1 Thessalonians 5:17-18). Brother Lawrence wrote, "I keep myself in His presence by simple attentiveness and a loving gaze upon God which I can call the actual presence of God or to put it more clearly, an habitual, silent and secret conversation of the soul with God."[10] Brother Lawrence discovered that practicing the presence of God led to moments of great joy, while not practicing God's presence led to just the opposite. He revealed, "The least turning away from Him is hell for me."[11]

"This side of heaven, life can be hell," I muttered as I crunched on a nondescript organic cracker to settle my stomach. Another wave of nausea disturbed my meditation—and my spirit. How realistic is it to try to meditate when I can hardly swallow a cracker? Aren't I asking too much of myself to practice the presence of God in a difficult moment such as this?

Then I reminded myself that I might be asking more of myself than God is asking of me. As Brother Lawrence wrote, "[God] does not ask much of us, merely a thought of Him from time to time, a little act of adoration, sometimes to ask for His grace, sometimes to offer Him your sufferings, at other times to thank Him for the graces, past and present, He has bestowed on you, in the midst of your troubles to take solace in Him as often as you can. . . . One need not cry out very loudly; He is nearer to us than we think."[12] It was relieving to remember that God's expectations for me were lower than mine were for myself. "Maybe that's because he knows me better than I know myself," I murmured, half smiling. As I washed the cracker crumbs from the plate, I found myself respecting the humble Brother Lawrence even more, for he was known to practice God's presence even when scrubbing pots and pans.

There will be no pots and pans tonight, I thought, as renewed nausea forced me back to bed. Then I had an idea. I may not be able to practice God's presence while washing dishes, but I can let his Word wash over me. I reached for my well-worn set of New Testament CDs in hopes of summoning God's healing presence by meditating on his Word.

Meditating on Scripture does not involve analyzing the verses but humbly receiving them. In being open to the Spirit of God in his Word, our relationship with him deepens, enabling us to more fully commune with him. I reached for Philippians, one of my favorite books of the New Testament. But halfway through I began to worry. Maybe I shouldn't have forced myself to eat. After all, some people believe that fasting aids in that communion.

People who fast report feeling closer to God. Some say they receive revelations. Others say they achieve a sense of well-being. Fasting heightens our sense of dependence upon God—the true Bread of Life—freeing us from baser earthly preoccupations. The veil, thickened by food and our desire for it, thins as we feast on God and are satisfied.

As a Jew, I was no stranger to fasting. Although asceticism is generally discouraged in Judaism, Jews may fast several times during the year, especially if they are Orthodox. For example, some fast on the Day of Lamentation, Tisha B'Av, which commemorates the destruction of the first and second Temples in Jerusalem. In addition to fasting in mourning, Jews have also fasted for petitionary purposes, although unlike Christians, they rarely do anymore. In biblical times, however, it was common for Jews to organize communal fasts as they called upon God to end a drought or protect them from an enemy. Today Jews fast mostly on Yom Kippur as penitence for sins committed as they make an accounting for their behavior in the year past. It is an opportunity not only to control physical appetites through self-denial but also to focus on the transcendent.

As a practicing Jew, my fasts on Yom Kippur produced a purity of heart and spirit unlike anything I had ever experienced, bringing me closer to God than at any other time of the year. I felt his presence even more acutely when, weak from hunger, I would stroll through the state park to shorten the long walk home from temple. In the clarity that fasting creates, every leaf glowed in the sunlight, every flower produced a rare radiance. It was a place between places.

Yet as I lay in bed remembering the physical weakness a fast can bring to a healthy body, I realized that even if I wanted to fast, my body would never make it past the thought. I turned over in bed and looked out the window at the magnificence of Pikes Peak. The mountain was glowing, backlit by a fiery, rose-colored sunset. Cumulous clouds hovering just above the peak brushed the iridescent rocky protrusions softly, rounding their edges. It was an eloquent answer to the agony of existence. Gazing through the window at the glowing, snowcapped peaks, my mind drifted back to better days in the mountains that now seemed so unreachable.

Only months before, I had climbed a mountain for the first time. The big balloon tires of my specially designed wheelchair escorted me easily over the trails, guided by my enthusiastic companion. It was fall, and the golden aspens quaked in the breeze, whispering their own distinctive song. As I was pushed higher and higher up the mountain, a rush of adrenaline sped through my body as I eagerly anticipated summiting. But just before we reached the peak, the terrain rose steeply, bringing us to a screeching halt. "Help me out of my chair. I want to climb the rest of the way," I requested. My friend stared at me doubtfully. "It's okay," I reassured her. "Help me up." Reaching for her hand, I slowly rose from my chair and, leaning heavily on her arm for support, set off to hike to the top.

"The heavens declare the glory of God; the skies proclaim the work of his hands," declared the psalmist (Psalm 19:1). I never fully appreciated those words until I reached the summit of that majestic mountain and saw the awesome sight. Stands of bright gold and orange aspens blanketed the distant peaks, their colors dripping over deep green patches of pine and fir trees like paint drizzled from a brush. A deep blue sky provided a dazzling backdrop for the magnificent canvas. Bright sunlight warmed my face as the gentle breeze cooled my body. It was amazing, not just to be standing in the midst of such beauty, but to be standing there at all. How miraculous that the mighty hand that had made everything as far as the eye could see had seen fit to take hold of my small, fragile hand through that of a friend. How incredible that I, who could barely walk, could actually summit for the first time in my life!

It wouldn't be the last time. I have traveled many mountain trails since then. Each time has been an affirmation of how glorious it is to achieve union with God in nature—and how exhilarating it is to experience the freedom that being united with him brings.

Unfortunately not even memories of that day, vibrant as they were, could rescue me from feeling trapped and lifeless as I lay in bed sick and alone, gazing at the world though a glass pane. I slumped back into the pillow and finally fell asleep, worlds away from the golden aspen leaves shimmering just outside my window.

When I awoke the next morning, still feeling ill, I had no idea how my life was about to change. It happened when a cherished friend who had just returned from a trip to Oregon came to visit, bearing an unusual gift. Shortly after her arrival, she reached into her black tote bag and pulled out a plastic bag filled with red and golden leaves. "Stand back!" she exclaimed as she snatched a big bunch of leaves from the bag. Raising her arms like a jubilant child, she tossed the leaves high into the air. As if falling gracefully from trees, they gently fluttered to the carpet, red and golden hues intertwining in a brilliant autumn dance. In the gentle wisp of air that stirred, I could feel the breath of God on my face.

"I wanted you to experience the falling of the autumn leaves," she said joyously. Tears trickled down my cheeks onto the beautiful leaves that surrounded me. I was mesmerized not only by how they had fluttered to the floor but also by their still-brilliant colors—steadfast remnants of the flush of life that had once coursed through their veins. Suddenly I felt life coursing through mine again.

It was not only the beauty of the sight that amazed me but also how it came to be. While I had spent the last several days suffering in bed, feeling ill and forgotten, my friend had been shuffling through newly fallen leaves under dazzling maple trees, picking the most colorful ones for me. She had protected the delicate treasures in plastic and pressed them into books when she arrived home so that no precious leaf would break, no color turn dull. Why had she been so careful to preserve a bunch of ordinary autumn leaves?

Maybe because her caring was anything but ordinary— it was an extraordinary mercy orchestrated by God. While she was meticulously selecting and preserving those leaves out of care for me, God was caring for me just as meticulously. Who else but the Lord would know so intimately

the desires of my heart that he would enlist a friend to
sprinkle leaves onto my carpet to bring me a miracle of
autumn? Who else would announce his loving presence in
the same palpable way I had experienced as a child sitting
in a maple tree among the rustling leaves, feeling his breath
on my face?

At that moment, I realized what had been missing in
my attempts to experience God's presence. It was not
God who wasn't present. What wasn't present was my
belief that he wanted to be. Divine encounters happen
because of *why* we are here. We are not only made for
relationship with each other. We are also made for relationship with God.

In fact, it is God, not us, who reaches out first and
keeps reaching out to us to the last. As Thomas Merton
wrote, "If you succeed in emptying your mind of every
thought and every desire, you may indeed withdraw into
the center of yourself and concentrate everything within
you upon the imaginary point where your life springs out of God: yet you will not really find God.
No natural exercise can
bring you into vital contact with Him. Unless He utters
Himself in you, speaks His own name in the center of
your soul, you will no more know Him than a stone
knows the ground upon which it rests in its inertia. Our
discovery of God is, in a way, God's discovery of us."[13]

I had spent the better part of the previous day going
through spiritual gymnastics to try to reach God. I had
practiced one discipline after another, believing that if I
could only perfect my methods, I could single-handedly
make an experience of God happen. Yet the more I tried,

It was not God who wasn't present but my belief that he wanted to be.

the less I felt his presence, because I had shifted my focus away from God and onto my own efforts. I had adopted a false sense of my own power while losing a real sense of his. It's not that I didn't believe God was powerful enough to create an encounter between him and me. It's just that I had forgotten how much he wants to. God speaks his name into our soul and sends his love into our heart because he yearns for relationship with us. We need only open our heart a crack to let his loving presence flood in.

Why would an omnipotent God want to meet us— mere fallen creatures in a fallen world? Why should he care whether or not we want to spend time with him? A powerful, omniscient God could run the universe just fine without us. Jesus didn't have to die on the cross, reaching out to us in saving grace. He didn't have to come from behind the veil that we put in place by our sin. In his final hours on earth, he didn't have to tear the curtain in two to restore our relationship with him. Why did he do all this for us? He did it because we were made for relationship with him.

We need only open our heart a crack to let his loving presence flood in.

Why do I continue to pray? Because I know that a loving God is with me working everything for the good. An indifferent God would most likely give us whatever we ask. It would be far easier for him to grant our requests than to deny them. But a loving God chooses, instead, to give us his best answer. He even loves us so much that at times he says no.

A loving God has also given us the Holy Spirit to guide us in our prayers, hoping that we will come to desire more and more what benefits us spiritually. As

Richard Foster reassures us, "God is not destroying the will but transforming it so that over a process of time and experience we can freely will what God wills. In the crucifixion of the will we are enabled to let go of our tight-fisted hold on life and follow our best prayers."[14] God hopes we will pray our best prayers. Yet he remains ever attentive to the unspoken desires of our heart.

When we fall to our knees in prayer, perched on the threshold between this life and the next, what do we desire most? We wish, first and foremost, for God to be with us. Mercifully that is the prayer he always grants. Just as he answered us long ago by coming to earth, he is answering us still every moment of every day simply and miraculously by being there in loving relationship with us.

Why should I empty myself, relinquishing myself to God? Because I know God loves me and wants to fill me with his presence. In fact, Jesus loves us so much that he emptied himself so that the power of God could work in him. Paul told us, "Your attitude should be the same as that of Christ Jesus: Who, being in very nature God, did not consider equality with God something to be grasped, but made himself nothing, taking the very nature of a servant, being made in human likeness. And being found in appearance as a man, he humbled himself and became obedient to death—even death on a cross!" (Philippians 2:5-8). Jesus could have called in legions of angels to avert his dreaded fate. Instead he submitted obediently to the will of the Father, praying, "If you are willing, take this cup from me; yet not my will, but yours be done" (Luke 22:42).

Why should I fall silent, believing that I will hear God's voice? Because Jesus talked to sinners, tax collectors, and outcasts, so why not to me? Jesus didn't concern himself just with creating masses of followers but forged a relationship with each person individually, especially the ones with whom others didn't. In reaching out to all of us, he demonstrated that he loves each of us too much not to embrace every one of us.

Why should I believe that if I practice the presence of God, Jesus will meet me in the muck and mire of my everyday life? Because he loved us enough to leave heaven to meet us in a fallen world. It would have been easier for God to stay in paradise or to show up exclusively in the beauty of a majestic cathedral. Jesus could have remained in the Temple, waiting for people to bow down at his feet. Instead he spent time with poor villagers, washing theirs. Maybe God is with us in every messy moment of our lives because he loves us too much to wait for Sunday.

Why should I meditate on God's Word? Because that's how a loving God speaks to us. In fact, his love is so great that he was willing to die to bring us the Word.

Why should I fast in hopes of encountering God? Because Jesus gave his body and blood for us—gifts we feast upon spiritually during Communion. Jesus said, "I tell you the truth, it is not Moses who has given you the bread from heaven, but it is my Father who gives you the true bread from heaven. For the bread of God is he who comes down from heaven and gives life to the world" (John 6:32-33). There is no greater love than this—that Jesus gave his life for us, even calling us his friends.

> *Maybe God is with us in every messy moment of our lives because he loves us too much to wait for Sunday.*

Why do I seek God's presence in nature? Because I know that a loving God desires to meet me there, escorting me up mountains when I can barely walk. He didn't have to make the world beautiful and give us five senses to enjoy it. Nor did he have to make Eden a paradise. He did it purely out of love.

John wrote, "We love because he first loved us" (1 John 4:19). Loving us first, God breathed himself into us before we could take a single breath. He came to earth to be the Answer to our prayers, and he answers our prayers still with his presence before we even ask. And in an act of ultimate sacrificial love, he died on the cross for us, forgiving us before we sin, giving us eternal life in his Kingdom before we enter heaven.

God can manifest himself in big displays or in subtle movements. It is up to us not to be so busy trying to make a divine encounter happen that we fail to notice that the one who loved us first is reaching out to us first in love.

Everything Jesus did, he did out of love. He could have performed spectacular miracles in front of the priests and teachers of the law. He could have stood outside the Temple gates like a magician pulling a rabbit out of a hat. Instead he used his powers, not for personal profit, but in the service of love. His healed us in love. He preached to us in love. He died for us in love. He rose in love, and he remains with us today, reaching out to us in love.

> God breathed himself into us before we could take a single breath.

Why do I, born and raised Jewish, believe that while lying in a sickbed, Jesus' presence actually came over me? It's because I know that what I was experiencing was not

110

some indifferent supernatural entity overtaking my body. It was the presence of a God who personally came to seek a relationship with me. Does that guarantee I will always experience his presence? Not necessarily. None of us can presume to understand the mysterious ways of communion with God. What we can know for certain, however, is that God loves us enough to move heaven and earth to reach us in this fallen world—in thin places.

Simone Weil wrote poignantly, "God wears himself out through the infinite thickness of time and space in order to reach the soul and to captivate it. If it allows a pure and utter consent (though brief as a lightning flash) to be torn from it, then God conquers that soul. . . . The soul, starting from the opposite end, makes the same journey that God made toward it. And that is the cross."[15]

The night of my friend's visit, I prayed in front of a wooden cross someone had given me when I first became a Christian. It spells out the name *Jesus* and has nails fastened to the back to symbolize his crucifixion. I prayed so fervently that I actually began to see a halo around the cross. It grew brighter and brighter until it shone with the most beautiful golden luminescence I had ever seen. It was as if God were responding to every syllable I prayed, every tear I shed. Or were the tears in my eyes causing the light to appear that way? I don't know.

What I do know for sure is *why* I am here. Jesus reaches out to me in miraculous ways every day because he lovingly made me for relationship with him. That is more than sufficient for me.

Chapter 9

We not only live in this world. We also live between this world and the next.

God seeks relationship with us in places of amazing thinness because he loves us. He demonstrated that love not only by dying to bring us from earth to heaven but also by living to bring us his Kingdom on earth. Jesus fills our lives with his love every day, hoping that we will do the same for each other because of *where* we are—in a thin place between this world and the next.

When I was sidelined from life, before I came to know Jesus, I found myself nowhere. My friends and colleagues went on with their busy lives, having little time for me. My mother's death soon thereafter left me feeling abandoned and alone. I spent my days watching others go to work while I was confined to a life of isolation and perpetual sick days. I was convinced that I was doomed to suffer a meaningless life, mattering to no one—not even myself.

Such thoughts are not unusual. They lurk deep within everyone's subconscious, threatening to emerge at the first sign of tragedy or weakness. I know this by the way people look at me when I'm in my wheelchair.

When I'm out in public, people often seem reticent to approach me. One day it dawned on me that maybe they are not really seeing me; they are visualizing themselves in my place. Some people may be afraid of me because of what I've become—but are they even more afraid of what might become of *them*? Is that why we work hard to achieve success, status, money, and fame—not just because we desire such things but also because we fear the alternative? Do we pass panhandlers on the street without making eye contact because we fear them or because we fear that we may hold that cup ourselves someday?

Growing up as the child of first-generation Jewish-American parents, I developed very specific beliefs about what defines success. My mother, who suffered from illness and poverty as a child, not only desired that her children have a better life, but she also feared what would happen if we didn't. Such feelings were typical of Jewish parents of her generation. The high standards they set for their children are the subject of many Jewish jokes. For example: "A Jewish mother is walking down the street with her two young sons. A passerby asks her how old the boys are. 'The doctor is three,' the mother answers. 'And the lawyer is two.'"[1] Or in a related joke: When does a Jewish embryo become a human being? The answer: After it graduates from medical school. Given my upbringing, it's not surprising that I would want to go far, all the way to becoming a Harvard-trained clinical psychologist.

In fact, how far I had come was the only thing on my mind the day I strolled the campus of a Harvard-affiliated teaching hospital for the first time. I'll never forget the feeling I had cavorting with the Ivy League elite. Not too many years earlier, Jews were still being excluded from such prestigious institutions. Now I was a member of the club, along with a few select others. Years later, when I was forced to quit my job, the insider became an outsider again. I would spend many years bemoaning my fate before realizing that being an outsider was the best preparation I could have had for becoming a follower of Jesus.

Yet in the years before I met Jesus, I spent countless moments railing against being sidelined as I battled my illness in a lonely struggle to survive. Daily life was grim. It was hard to sit up and read, so I watched TV until I became bored. Finally I discovered books on tape. It was hard to digest food and my weight was down to eighty-seven pounds, so my doctor placed me on baby formula, which I sipped through a straw. As I faced formidable physical trials all alone, every minute felt like an hour, every hour felt like an eternity. Now the time I'd never seemed to have enough of before was too much for me. Time literally hurt. Not only did I find myself nowhere, there seemed to be nowhere to go and no way out.

Unfortunately all I knew of Jesus at the time was my mother's admonition that I must never know him. I dared not even speak the name of Jesus, whom my mother blamed for instigating centuries of Jewish persecution, including the deaths of most of her maternal relatives in the pogroms. In desperation, I turned to the God of my upbringing. Unfortunately he, like everyone around me, seemed distant and uncaring. I was not surprised. He had never been a personal God but an unreachable deity who delivered the law from above to the multitudes, as he did on Mount Sinai—not like Jesus, who offers grace to each of us here below. In an effort to connect with God and with my fellow Jews, I contacted a local conservative synagogue and made an appointment to speak with a rabbi.

Exhausted from making the trip, I sat in the rabbi's small, cluttered office, summoning the little energy I had left to explain, "I'd like to find a way to feel connected to God and Judaism. I'm homebound much of the time and wonder whether there is a congregant who could visit me and maybe even teach me more about Judaism." The rabbi looked at me sympathetically and told me he'd get back to me. He never did.

Undaunted, I called a second temple and arranged a meeting with a female rabbi. After another arduous trip and a similar discussion, I did get a call back, but the news wasn't good. In a dispassionate tone, she informed me that she could find no one to help me. "But if you can ever come to regular Torah study, you are welcome," she said. I couldn't, so I didn't.

Instead I sank deeper and deeper into despair, feeling even more discouraged. In my frustration, I chastised myself. Hadn't my parents taught me not to expect something for nothing? Hadn't my competitive New York upbringing shown me you have to work for everything you get? Why should I expect someone to help me now? I had just about given up reaching out to God—or anyone else—when I had an idea. If I could find a way to obtain a computer, I could go online and take a course on Judaism.

I contacted the Jewish Federation, hoping that such a well-endowed charitable organization could help me track down an outdated model that had been discarded in favor of a new one. I knew that the Jewish community had a well-organized network of charities. In fact, I had heard friends complain that once they gave to one charity, they received constant hounding from a multitude of others. Albert Vorspan, author of *Start Worrying: Details to Follow*, quips, "To disassociate effectively" from Jewish solicitation, "you have to enter an FBI Witness Relocation Program and adopt a new identity."[2] Jews may joke and even complain about giving, yet when compared to the rest of society, they contribute far more to charity. Judaism has always emphasized tzedakah. In fact, it is said that tzedakah is equal to all other commandments combined.

With high expectations, I contacted the Jewish Federation and explained my situation to the woman who took my call. She was less than sympathetic, cutting me off abruptly and referring me to another agency. I immediately dialed that number, only to be told that they donate computers exclusively to organizations. So far all the responses I had received were as impersonal as the God I was supposed to worship.

Finally I turned to a cousin who was a practicing Jew for advice. I figured that he might have an "in," either with God or his people. Unfortunately he had neither. He was brief and to the point: "It's not that Jews don't do mitzvahs," he said. "Judaism has a long tradition emphasizing charity. It's just that Jews nowadays are more into donating to organizations. You know, Beverly, if you want personal help, maybe you should go to Christians."

"Sure," I said dismissively, thinking he was being facetious. Neither one of us had any idea at the time how prophetic his words would be.

Some time later, feeling lost and abandoned, I would turn to a little book about Jesus and, upon reading it, whisper his name, ushering him into my life. Only by grace did I find that unexpected door. "Find the door of your heart, you will discover it is the door of the kingdom of God,"[3] said Saint John Chrysostom. In discovering that door and opening it just a crack, I not only found out who God really is in Jesus, I also discovered where I really was.

I doubt my Jewish relative would have approved of my finding myself not only with Jesus but also in his Kingdom. To this day, when we discuss my conversion, he always asks, "How could you accept Jesus as the Messiah when he certainly didn't make this world a paradise?" His question comes right out of Old Testament times.

When Jesus spoke the first recorded words of his ministry—"The kingdom of heaven is near" (Matthew 4:17) —his earthshaking announcement should have been good news to everyone. After all, God had finally broken into history to inaugurate his rule. Yet when Jesus offered the Kingdom to the Jews, knowing that they were the proper heirs, the religious leaders rebuked him and prevented others from accepting him. Why would first-century Jews, who had been praying for the coming of the Messiah, not have jumped for joy at his arrival? Why wasn't the gospel good news to a people who had waited so long for the promised Kingdom of God? It was the same reason my cousin gave me for not accepting Jesus. The Jews believed then, as they do now, that the Messiah would bring peace to all the earth.

When I first accepted Jesus, I knew that the Kingdom he had come to inaugurate was "now" but "not yet." However, the moment I felt the peace of Christ for the first time, I knew I had finally arrived where I was meant to be. Some would accuse me of settling in desperation for a false Messiah. I know better, for the incredible peace that I experienced in Jesus that day was real—a divine deposit until his Kingdom on earth will be fully realized.

Soon after Jesus personally came to me, so did those who worshipped and served a personal God, literally changing my life. It was not because of who I was that they reached out to me. It was because of *where* we were.

It happened more times than I can recount. The first time occurred only weeks after I became a Christian. I had placed an advertisement for an apartment to rent in a neighboring church's newsletter, and a woman named Gail responded. After conversing with me for several minutes, she offered to have her women's Bible study group pray for me. I was taken aback and a little suspicious. *Why would her Bible group want to pray for someone they don't even know? I wondered. I live a meaningless life in which even I don't think I matter. Why should I matter to them? Besides, I have nothing to give them in return.* I hesitated for a long moment before answering Gail. Then before I could say no, I said yes, more out of desperation than belief.

The incredible peace I experienced in Jesus was real—a divine deposit until his Kingdom on earth will be fully realized.

Several days later, something unexpected and truly amazing happened. I began receiving inspirational cards from members of her group. Each time another card arrived, I was perplexed but found myself taping it to the wall facing my bed nevertheless. Within a short time the entire wall was filled with cards. As I lay in bed, staring at the array of greetings from well-wishers I didn't even know, I felt surprisingly comforted and encouraged. Their thoughts and prayers sustained me in ways I could never have imagined—nor could they ever know.

Still the question remained: Why would an entire group of strangers care about somebody they had never even met—a nobody who was nowhere, cast aside from the mainstream? What was in it for them? I turned to the Bible.

As I began to read about the life of Jesus, I learned that the Lord was no fan of the mainstream I was so eager to rejoin. It didn't trouble him that he had been banished when he had refused to hobnob with the powerful and elite, for he preferred to commune with those in need: the ill, the outcasts, the sinners. He even chose to break the rules, such as performing healing on the Sabbath, for which he was mercilessly chastised. His words and actions were considered so subversive that they eventually cost him his life. Reading about the love and sacrifice of Jesus for the sick and forgotten made me weep. Yet I still wondered, *Even if God does love me, why would he come all the way to earth to challenge the status quo and inaugurate his Kingdom?* I found the answer in an unexpected place.

In his book *Albert Camus and the Minister*, Pastor Howard Mumma relates a story he told to the philosopher Camus: "I recall a wise man saying to a friend, 'The whole trouble in our world is the lack of an apostrophe.' When the friend wanted to know what he meant, he said, 'Well look at Adoph Hitler and at Mussolini and at Josef Stalin and at Hideki Tojo—What you see is this: men trying to be gods instead of trying to be God's.'"[4]

Suddenly I understood. In love, Jesus had come to earth to claim us as his own—to gather his flock in a fallen world and give us shelter, sustenance, and saving grace in his Kingdom before taking us home. It matters not to Jesus who we are in worldly terms of money, success, and prestige. It matters only that we are his and, consequently, rightful citizens of his Kingdom.

The women in Gail's group had reached out to me because, as Kingdom dwellers, they knew that we not only live in this world. We live between this world and the next—in God's Kingdom.

Why did they give of themselves to me—a poor, bereft nobody? Because Jesus said, "Blessed are the poor in spirit, for theirs is the kingdom of heaven" (Matthew 5:3). It is the poor in spirit, those who have nothing to give God, who need his saving grace. We are to value them as much as Jesus does.

Why did they send me cards filled with compassionate wishes and heartfelt prayers? Because Jesus said, "Blessed are the merciful, for they will be shown mercy" (Matthew 5:7). What is mercy? It is compassion for people in need.

Why did they have no expectation of reciprocation? Because Jesus said, "Blessed are the pure in heart, for they will see God" (Matthew 5:8). They are blessed whose thoughts and motives are pure.

Why didn't even one of the women call me to claim credit for her good deed? Because Jesus said, "Blessed are the meek, for they will inherit the earth" (Matthew 5:5). They are blessed who have a gentle, humble attitude, leading to a true estimate of oneself.

Why didn't they just sit back and do nothing to help me, as so many others had done? Because Jesus said, "You are the salt of the earth. But if the salt loses its saltiness, how can it be made salty again?" (Matthew 5:13). True Christians strive to retain their true Christian character and not allow themselves to be contaminated by selfish, worldly desires.

Why did those women strive to bring light to my darkened existence? Because Jesus said, "You are the light of the world. A city on a hill cannot be hidden. Neither do people light a lamp and put it under a bowl. Instead they put it on its stand, and it gives light to everyone in the house. In the same way, let your light shine before men, that they may see your good deeds and praise your Father in heaven" (Matthew 5:14-16). Christians allow the light of God to shine through them to others, glorifying him.

When Jesus came to inaugurate the Kingdom, he instituted a counterculture where the humble would be exalted, the last would be first, and the meek would be heirs to the earth. In the process, he not only turned the tables on the establishment but also turned the world upside down—inaugurating the Kingdom of heaven on earth. It was nothing short of revolutionary. As Richard Foster said, "Jesus was, and is, a social revolutionary. When he healed the sick, he did more than cure diseases: he healed the sickness in a society that would cast these people aside. When he pronounced his beatitudes upon the people, he was taking up those classes and categories that society deemed to be unblessed and unblessable. He told these 'sat upon, spat upon, ratted on' people that they were precious in the kingdom of God. He blessed the children; he talked with an outcast woman; he hob-nobbed with a wealthy crook."[5] Jesus came to teach us to live as contrary to the fallen world's standards as he did— in the transcendent Kingdom he had come to inaugurate.

Jesus made it clear that his Kingdom was not of this world. He had not come to earth to conquer armies and end Roman occupation but to win the peace, one trans-formed heart at a time. The new life he offered was not rescue from a fallen world but redemption for the fallen. "Repent, for the kingdom of heaven is near" (Matthew 4:17), Jesus proclaimed, offering the Kingdom to all who would humbly repent and accept him. It was not life in a changed world but a new life born of the Spirit in a changed heart where God can reside. We can see Jesus in the hearts of Christians today—if we know where to look.

There is no one I know who evidences a heart filled with God's love more than Pastor Dave. Dave and I first made contact only a week after I accepted Jesus. I had told my friend Lynne the news of my conversion, and she suggested that I call her good friend Pastor Dave. It was several days before I summoned the courage to phone him, because I had never spoken to a pastor before and didn't know quite what to say. Finally I nervously made the call. Much to my amazement, as soon as I heard Dave's voice, my fears melted. His warmth and caring made me feel as if I was talking to a beloved brother.

> Jesus not only turned the tables on the establishment but also turned the world upside down—inaugurating the Kingdom of heaven on earth.

Dave visited me later that week, and shortly after the visit he began speaking about me from the pulpit on Sundays. His stories generated such interest that many congregants asked if they could meet me. Unfortunately I was so ill that I couldn't attend church. Dave pondered the seemingly unsolvable dilemma until he finally came up with an ingenious solution. He would find a way to rig up a loudspeaker system and attach it to a telephone.

Several weeks later I did what I thought would never be possible. I attended church from the confines of my bed, speaking to the entire congregation via telephone. Not only had the body of Christ reached me in my soli-

123

tude, but they had also found a way for me to reach them. For hours thereafter, I lay in bed alone, reliving those precious moments in my mind, knowing that in reality I was not alone.

Making Dave's acquaintance right after I met Jesus convinced me more than anything of the truth of Jesus, because I could see Jesus in Dave's heart. In fact, being with Dave always reminds me that while we may be in the world, we were never meant to be of it.

As Christians, we are citizens of a Kingdom on the ethereal edge between this world and the next—in a thin place. Our true home is not here but in a far different place, for we are born of God and will return to him. We may live our lives looking forward to heaven, but we also look backward from it: seeing ourselves through God's eyes, not our own; living by faith, not by sight.

I'll never forget the movie *E.T.* In a classic scene, E.T. tries to make a device to signal the spaceship that left without him, all the while mumbling, "E.T. phone home." When I pray, I sometimes think, *BJ* [my nickname] *phone home.* Yet unlike E.T., we need not signal our home base. God knows where we are. He only hopes that, as Kingdom dwellers, we remember where we are.

We are citizens of a Kingdom on the ethereal edge between this world and the next—in a thin place.

As citizens of the Kingdom, we are to model ourselves after Jesus—a King who was a servant, for he asks no less of us. As Jesus said, "If anyone wants to be first, he must be the very last, and the servant of all" (Mark 9:35). Just as Jesus spent his life in service, we are called to adopt service as a lifestyle, submitting not only to God but also to each other. In the process, we free ourselves from the tyranny of our own needs to value the hopes and dreams of others.

As I came to know Dave better, I was struck by his steadfast commitment to service. He reached out not only to me in my solitude but also to many others who were alone in the world. For years he had kept in touch with a prisoner who, because of Dave's faithful visits, had become a Christian in prison. Often Dave would read Steve's poignant letters from prison to the congregation. It was clear that while Steve's body may have been imprisoned, his soul had been freed. Dave had also kept in touch with a fireman who tragically had contracted Lou Gehrig's disease in his forties. John had not been much of a believer, but Dave was undaunted. When no one else would visit, Dave was there, literally to the end. Dave was also there for an old congregant who could no longer attend church. An avid Red Sox fan, Mary had always told Dave that she wouldn't die until the Red Sox were victorious. After the Red Sox won the World Series, Dave visited Mary in the nursing home. There she sat, at the age of ninety-three, restrained to a chair, barely able to communicate, receiving with joy Dave's gift of a Red Sox World Series championship cup.

Serving others may not always be an easy task, but fortunately we need not bear these burdens alone. We can lay them at the feet of Jesus, who beckons to the burdened and weary to find rest in him.

It would be wonderful if all we needed to do is rest in Jesus. Yet as members of a divine Kingdom, straddling the ethereal border between this world and the next, we are called to do far more than rest. As Philip Yancey observes, "Jesus offers a peace that involves new turmoil, a rest that involves new tasks. The 'peace of God, which transcends all understanding' promised in the New Testament is a peace in the midst of warfare, a calmness in the midst of fear, a confidence in the midst of doubt. Living as resident aliens in a strange land, citizens of a secret kingdom, what other kind of peace should we expect? In this world restlessness, and not contentment, is a sign of health."[6]

The war rages on between good and evil, and we are foot soldiers on the front lines in a cosmic battle. How can we, as mere fallen mortals, begin to fight the overwhelming evil in this fallen world? We can if we begin with ourselves, actively turning toward God to repent of our sins, while turning away from our own petty concerns to help others. In committing ourselves to doing God's will, we can serve as God's instruments, helping to make his Kingdom on earth a living, breathing reality in our lives and the lives of others.

It is our choice to make. We may choose to follow the crowd or a higher power. We may make ourselves the center of our universe or make God our center. We may become enamored solely with the things of this world or choose what endures in eternity. We may strive for success, money, and fame for our own glory, or we may use them for the glory of God. We may love like mere humans or learn to love like God loves, not with self-interest, but with the selfless love of Jesus Christ.

I experienced that love again several years ago, when shortly before Christmas, I received a letter in the mail from my church regarding the Christmas offering. As I read it, I was surprised to find that it was about my need for a computer. A month later, Dave called, telling me that the congregation had raised almost six thousand dollars to buy me "the best computer money could buy." My heart was so full of gratitude that I could hardly speak. If I could have spoken, however, I know I would not have asked why the congregation had given me such a generous gift. I already knew.

By grace, Jesus will return to establish the undisputed reign of God forever. For now, we live between this world and the next. How much easier it would be to proceed directly to heaven rather than toil in his Kingdom on earth, where we are called to be light in the midst of darkness. How hard it is to stand up for what is right in a fallen world, when the moral fabric of society seems to be unraveling all around us.

We strive to confidently fight the good fight, in Jesus. We struggle to strike a balance in our hectic lives as we endeavor to make a good home in this far-from-perfect world—far

> *We may love like mere humans or learn to love like God loves, not with self-interest, but with the selfless love of Jesus Christ.*

from our true home. It's far from easy. Some of us may be tempted to ask, "What's the point of remaining here when it's so much better there?" Peter Kreeft may offer the best answer: "The point of our lives in this world is not comfort, security, or even happiness, but training; not fulfillment but preparation. It's a lousy home, but it's a fine gymnasium. . . . For we misunderstand where we are if we believe in earthly utopias. The universe is a soul-making machine, a womb, an egg. Jesus didn't make it into a rose garden when he came, though he could have. Rather, he wore the thorns from this world's gardens."[7]

In this world we may have trouble, but we can take heart, for God is with us in our struggle for peace and justice, and he will prevail. Jesus overcame the world, and so will we—in him.

We do not have to wait for that final victory in order for us to be victorious, however. We can win every day by becoming a thin place for each other, allowing the loving light of God to shine through us. The veil between heaven and earth thins every time we love each other as ourselves; reach out to the lonely, sick, poor, and forgotten; place the needs of others above our own; and answer evil with good. And what is most amazing is that we who give are the ones who are most blessed.

We can win every day by becoming a thin place for each other, allowing the loving light of God to shine through us.

For when we reach out to all in love, we affirm that, as citizens of God's Kingdom, each one of us matters—no matter what.

PART III
How in Heaven's Name I Became a Thin Place

Chapter 10

My Father and Me—and the Son?

God not only shines his light upon us. He also shines his light through us to others.

Human history begins and ends in a thin place. In between we live in an in-between kingdom, yearning to recapture what was lost. It is a loss we have grieved ever since Adam and Eve sinned, violating their perfect union with God—a loss that God moved heaven and earth to restore.

In Old Testament times, God stepped into history frequently, not only to make his presence known, but also to make known his wish to mend our broken relationship with him. Unfortunately his attempts largely fell on deaf ears. Under the covenantal system of rewards and punishments, disobedience and even anarchy reigned because our sin continued to stand in the way.

Finally God came in forgiveness, bridging the chasm that separated us from him. In Jesus, intimacy was made possible again, not only because God could be experienced up close and personal. Not only because spirit and matter were joined in him, unifying creation. But also because Jesus bore our sins, reconciling us to God. What could not be achieved through the rule of law, God achieved through his sacrificial love in the suffering of Jesus Christ. In a new covenant of grace and forgiveness, the barrier between a holy God and his sinful creation was forever removed, thinning the veil and restoring our access to him. We need only repent, believe, and extend the gift to others.

Paul said, "Be kind and compassionate to one another, forgiving each other, just as in Christ God forgave you" (Ephesians 4:32). Just as Christ forgave us so that we could be reconciled to the Father, he expects us to do the same for each other.

This may be easier said than done, especially when it comes to reconciling with an earthly father. Yet it was only when I found a way to forgive my own father that something miraculous happened. The thinnest of places materialized—within me.

Growing up, I envied the children on the television sitcoms of the 1950s, whose dads arrived home from work in the light of day. These fatherly heroes would burst through the front door, fresher than when they left, eager to listen to blow-by-blow descriptions of the happenings of the day. No problem was too small to be solved by these self-appointed sitcom Solomons, who had the patience of a saint.

When my father finally made it home from our ghetto store, it was dark. Arriving home alive was a feat in itself, even though he usually appeared half dead. Dad would brush by me, bleary-eyed and not so bushy-tailed, wolf down a quick dinner in front of the television, and turn in for bed. He never met the idyllic dads of my sitcoms.

They had long since retired at a more respectable hour. Although had my dad encountered those unflappable fathers, he probably would have changed the channel. Dad was into reality TV way before its time.

It's not as if my father and I never spent time together. I was recruited at age ten to work in the store, where I spent weekends and holidays learning more than I cared to know about the finer points of baby buntings and brassieres. And then there was always the inevitable seasonal bonding at home for the sake of summer lawn care and autumn leaves, even though the focus was on lawn fungus, not fourth grade. That's because my father rarely engaged with anybody in a meaningful way—except when playing his ukulele.

My dad's claim to fame was a short stint with the Harmonicats at the Loews and RKO theaters in New York City. They were a harmonica band that featured a little guy with a big harmonica—and a whole lot of wind, apparently. After ten grueling weeks, my father never worked in the music business again. "Musicians are bums," he once explained to me. Apparently, he didn't much like the little guy with the big harmonica.

After that Dad limited himself to performing for relatives at weddings and bar mitzvahs. When my father heard the first squeaks of "Hava Nagila" emanating from my fourth grade loaner clarinet, I was recruited for the act.

By the time I was in my thirties, my father was retired in Florida, making quite a name for himself entertaining at nursing homes and retirement villages. I was invited to come along whenever I visited from Boston. Often I would stand in the back of the room and watch him perform solo before joining in with my clarinet.

My father's signature act was dressing up like a woman and singing "Hello, Dolly" while sporting a very curly, very red wig. Even the most comatose nursing home patients seemed to perk up at the sight of this ukulele-strumming senior citizen strutting around singing show tunes in drag. I must admit that it was a little unnerving to be related to an eighty-year-old cross-dresser. Nevertheless, I was proud of my father's valiant efforts to bring joy to forgotten, lonely souls. He seemed to relish reaching out to those in need. Which left me wondering: Why not to me?

While my father undoubtedly loved me, he never paid much attention to me. When he did, I often wished he hadn't, for he could be harsh and sometimes even cruel—not physically, but emotionally. My emotions remained raw all the way into adulthood about the hurtful way my father had treated me.

It wasn't as if my father wasn't a good guy. He was. In fact, he had a good heart and showed his love in many ways. It's just that he had never learned how to be a good father from his own father, who apparently wasn't one.

That's why my feelings erupted in a fury the day my father turned to me for help. He had fallen ill with progressive heart disease, and having nowhere else to go, he called me. "I'm having trouble getting medical services, and I need your help," he lamented. I told him I'd see what I could do. As I hung up the phone, I felt a surge of anger well up in me, ushering in second thoughts. Did I really want to reconcile with my father after all these years, especially after all he had done?

As I struggled to contain my anger after his call, my mind flooded with troubling memories of a night I wished I could forget.

I was ten years old when I found a lost kitten several blocks from my house. It looked like a little white fur ball with black spots. I sat for hours holding it ever so gently in my lap, stroking its soft fur while it purred loudly. When my mother said I could keep it, I was overjoyed. When my father came home, however, he snapped into action, ordering my brother to grab the kitten and take it to the car. Driving to a remote location, he demanded that Ed abandon the kitten on a lonely road. I cried for a week.

Memories of the pain of that night caused tears to flow after my father's unexpected call. I couldn't believe that after so many years I still felt the hurt. Nor could I erase from my mind the image of a helpless kitten being left alone to perish. Soon other flashbacks took its place. I saw my father throwing out every one of my toys because I hadn't cleaned up my room. Then I remembered his threatening to throw me out shortly after I returned home, suffering with this disease. Not long after my mother died, he had walked into my room emotionally distraught and issued an ultimatum: "Pick yourself up by your boot-straps. I'll give you three months." Even though I knew he had said it in a fit of anger and would never have enforced the deadline, I dragged myself out of bed and moved back to Boston, hoping to find a way to make it on my own.

I walked away then, so why shouldn't I walk away now? Then, remembering my psychological training, I thought, *Maybe I should try to understand why my father can be so harsh, so that I can more easily forgive him. After all, he faced tough times in his life. He survived street fights as a child in the Bronx, the Great Depression, World War II, and numerous life-threatening robberies in his store, which was located in a racially troubled section of Brooklyn. He was slapped by his abusive father for seeking even a modicum of attention from him. He was regularly beaten up by his older brother. As a stutterer, he was taunted by neighborhood kids and was self-conscious of his speech impediment well into adulthood. Maybe that's why Dad became toughened and lashes out at times—because he is convinced that the world is a dangerous place where he can't trust anyone or allow anyone to get too close—even his own family.*

Yet understanding why didn't bring me any closer to forgiving my father. Nor did it really matter. Forgiveness does not require that we understand, only that we forgive even when we don't understand. How do I know?

As I was about to walk away, I suddenly remembered Someone who had unconditionally forgiven me. How could I not work to reconcile with my father when Jesus had died on the cross to reconcile me to the Father?

Turning to the Bible, I read that when Jesus walked the earth, he not only asked that we forgive one another but also asked that we forgive without judgment or condemnation. "Do not judge, and you will not be judged. Do not condemn, and you will not be condemned. Forgive, and you will be forgiven," Jesus told us (Luke 6:37). Perusing the pages describing his crucifixion, I made a startling discovery. On the cross, Jesus did not pronounce judgment upon his persecutors. He did not condemn them for what they were about to do. Even when lashed to the splintering wood, sweat pouring from his brow, body aching

Forgiveness does not require that we understand, only that we forgive even when we don't understand.

from hours of torture, blood dripping from nail holes in his flesh, he proclaimed, "Father, forgive them, for they do not know what they are doing" (Luke 23:34). It was one of the most astonishing statements of grace in history.

Such amazing forgiveness did not end with Jesus' death on the cross. In fact, it only began there. For centuries thereafter, Christian martyrs were known to actually pray for their persecutors, as Stephen, the first martyr, prayed before his execution: "Lord, do not hold this sin against them" (Acts 7:60).

If Jesus and his followers could forgive in such egregious circumstances, why couldn't I forgive my father? If Jesus died to reconcile us to the Father, why couldn't I find a way to reconcile with my earthly father? I struggled hard to come up with an answer until I finally thought I had it. Maybe I was having such a hard time forgiving because my mother had taught me that some things are unforgivable.

My mother had never forgiven the murderers of her family. Neither had I, especially since their murderous acts had indirectly killed my mother. Because her parents were so poor after they were forced to flee Russia, my mother's rheumatic fever went untreated, leaving her with a permanent heart valve defect. Later in life, that valve closed, causing her to die right in front of me before I revived her with CPR. Only three weeks later, complications from surgery to repair that valve ultimately killed her.

It was devastating to lose my mother that way, especially since at age seventy-two she was otherwise healthy. Yet just because she had not forgiven the murderers of her family didn't mean that I shouldn't forgive them. Hadn't other Jews long since forgiven their persecutors?

I thought back to an eerie encounter that happened long ago, which made the question all too real.

As a teenager, I visited a temple in Amsterdam. My brother and I had been sightseeing when we came upon a building with a small Jewish star under the eaves. It was located in the midst of a maze of highways. Ed and I decided to enter the temple and look around. As we did, we spied a sullen young man at the back of the sanctuary. He explained, "This used to be a thriving Jewish community until, one day during worship, the Nazis came and rounded up every one of the congregants, shipping them to concentration camps. Afterward they bulldozed the houses, so that no sign of the neighborhood remained. Even now, few Jews live around here." His eyes filled with tears as he told us that he was the rabbi of the congregation. *A congregation comprised mostly of the dearly departed*, I thought. A chill ran down my spine. If my brother and I had been standing in that very spot less than three decades earlier, we ourselves would have been dragged away and probably killed.

As I remembered that day, I wondered if my mother was right. Maybe some sins are unforgivable. Would Jesus really expect me to forgive under any circumstances, even such horrific crimes perpetrated on innocent Jews? I found an answer in a most unexpected place—the writings of a devout Christian.

Corrie ten Boom, a Christian who had been arrested by the Nazis and deported to Ravensbrück for hiding Jews, survived the war, only to face a torturous personal struggle of the heart. She was delivering one of her postwar speeches emphasizing Jesus' message of forgiveness, when she came face-to-face with one of her torturers from the camp. She wrote:

One moment I saw the overcoat and the brown hat; the next, a blue uniform and a visored cap with its skull and crossbones. It came back with a rush: the huge room with its harsh overhead lights; the pathetic pile of dresses and shoes in the center of the floor; the shame of walking naked past this man. . . . Now he was in front of me, hand thrust out: "A fine message, Fraulein! How good it is to know that, as you say, all our sins are at the bottom of the sea!" And I, who had spoken so glibly of forgiveness, fumbled in my pocketbook rather than take that hand. He would not remember me, of course—how could he remember one prisoner among those thousands of women? But I remembered him and the leather crop swinging from his belt. I was face-to-face with one of my captors and my blood seemed to freeze.[1]

He told her that he had become a Christian and knew God had forgiven him for his cruelty. Yet she could not bring herself to forgive him. She lamented:

And I stood there—I whose sins had again and again to be forgiven—and could not forgive. Betsie [Corrie's sister] had died in that place—could he erase her slow terrible death simply for the asking? It could not have been many seconds that he stood there—hand held out—but to me it seemed hours as I wrestled with the most difficult thing I had ever had to do. For I had to do it—I knew that. The message that God forgives has a prior condition: that we forgive those who have injured us. . . . And so woodenly, mechanically, I thrust my hand into the one stretched out to me. And as I did, an incredible thing took place. The current started in my shoulder, raced down my arm, sprang into our joined hands. And then this healing warmth seemed to flood my whole being, bringing tears to my eyes. "I forgive you, brother!" I cried. "With all my heart." For a long moment we grasped each other's hands, the former guard and the former prisoner. I had never known God's love so intensely, as I did then."[2]

What was the healing warmth that Corrie ten Boom felt at the moment she forgave her torturer? Or rather who was it coming through the veil, in the thinness of forgiveness? Had I felt it too, not because I forgave, but because I was forgiven?

At the very moment the pastor had placed the sign of the cross on my forehead on the day of my baptism, a healing warmth flooded my body. There I sat, a Christian friend holding my right hand and my Jewish brother holding my left, feeling that amazing warmth flowing through my hands into theirs. A stream of light coming through the stained-glass windows high above our heads bathed us in a luminescent glow as it shone upon us all— Christian and Jew alike. I felt like jumping for joy, right out of my wheelchair, to dance in the warmth of that light. For in that place between heaven and earth, God had come through the veil to bathe us in his love. At the moment of my baptism, he had come to me again in for- giveness, despite my lack of goodness, to sweep me in his arms so that I could belong to him for good. Reverend Peter Gomes waxes eloquent about the miracle of bap- tism: "We share in the baptism of Jesus and by that we are renewed, regenerated, called back to the life we were meant to live when we first were created, for when God had done with us the first time he said that it and we were good, and he doesn't rest until he gets us back."[3]

I am forgiven and should forgive. That's what I told

myself as I struggled to respond to my father's call for
help. If God suffered and died to reconcile us to him, why
shouldn't I find a way to
reconcile with my father?
That is the message of
Jesus. Yet what if my father
is unrepentant? I asked
myself. How can I forgive
someone who doesn't think he needs forgiveness? The
answer may rest in a note found near the body of a dead
concentration camp child.

In that place between heaven and earth, God had come through the veil to bathe us in his love.

In his book *Prayer*, Richard Foster relates the following poignant words that were scrawled on a piece of
wrapping paper found near a deceased child in Ravensbrück:

> O Lord, remember not only the men and women of
> good will, but also those of ill will. But do not only
> remember the suffering they have inflicted on us;
> remember the fruits we bought, thanks to this suffering:
> our comradeship, our loyalty, our humility, the courage,
> the generosity, the greatness of heart which has grown
> out of all this. And when they come to judgment, let all
> the fruits that we have borne be their forgiveness.[4]

If those noble concentration camp victims, who faced
imminent death, could pray for those who transgressed
against them, why couldn't I? Why couldn't I pray for my
father in hopes that he would eventually repent and turn
to God? After all, forgiving doesn't mean that sin doesn't
matter. We are called to love the sinner, not the sin. Just
as by grace Jesus loves us despite our sins. Jesus should
know. He had more forgiving to do than anyone else in

history. Yet he demonstrated that love is greater than any offense. Love can bridge any chasm and mend the most broken of relationships.

I finally forgave my father, calling him back to offer my help whenever he needed it. For years I worked relentlessly to keep home services in place so that my father could remain in his own apartment to the very end. That was a gift to a man who had always feared living in a nursing home more than he feared death, because his mother had died in one.

It wasn't a one-way street, however. Together we worked hard in the remaining years to mend our relationship and achieve lasting reconciliation. It began when I started listening to my father with the grace and compassion of Jesus. And surprisingly my father started listening to me. Every time we talked, our love and respect for each other grew. As Dad found himself struggling with illness on a daily basis, he became more empathetic and supportive of my battle with disease. Soon we were talking almost every day, sharing our deepest feelings, hopes, and dreams. Then something amazing happened.

I received a special present in the mail. Opening the package, I found a picture of my father's choral group. I searched in vain to locate my father in the photo, until I realized that he was the curly-haired redhead in the floral dress with the big microphone. Then I felt something else in the tissue paper. As I pushed the crumpled paper aside, I discovered a lovely handmade doll in an orange crocheted dress with a note attached: "Enjoy. . . . Love, Dad." Tearfully I placed her on my shelf, knowing that this was one doll that would never be thrown out. I named her Grace.

As time passed, I summoned the courage to tell my

father about the love and grace of Jesus. I fully expected to be ignored or chastised, but much to my amazement, he did not turn away. In fact, when friends asked him if he would like a visit from clergy, he requested a pastor. I was stunned and delighted, especially since they found him a ukulele-playing pastor who had just moved to Florida from Hawaii. When my father told me, I laughed, thinking, *Such is the meticulous attention to detail and sense of humor of our Lord.* Eventually that pastor moved away and was replaced by another, who would form a lasting bond not only with Dad but also with Ed and me.

That was a blessing, since my father lingered for a long time in failing health. Those of us who knew him were beginning to wonder whether the inevitable might not be so inevitable. Every time he took a turn for the worse, it turned out he got better. My brother began referring to him as the "boy who cried wolf," because Dad had escaped the jaws of death so many times. How long could a ninety-three-year-old man with advanced heart disease live, we wondered, especially one with an abdominal aortic aneurysm that was ballooning bigger by the minute? Later I realized that my father had to find a way to live before he could find a way to die.

Dad finally died in January 2004, just after the start of the New Year. Even though I knew he couldn't hang on forever, I was still devastated. The day after my father's death, I received a call from the pastor. I had expected his call, but I never could have expected what he was about to say.

After expressing his condolences, he told me, "Your dad's nurse gave him a book about Jesus last week, and he read it."

"That's surprising," I responded. "I sent my father

several books like that, and he said they bored him."
"Well, he read this one," he replied with a lift in his
voice. "He loved you with all his heart, you know,
Beverly. He would have given his life for you." I began
to cry. He continued, "You were so firm in your faith. It
almost didn't leave him an option." Suddenly my grief
began to turn to disbelief. Was he saying what I thought
he was saying? "I knew the Lord would work in his
life," he told me. "The book only changed him because
of what you said; it summarized what you had been saying over the years. He told me, 'Now I'm getting what
Beverly is talking about. What Beverly has talked about
all the time. Now I get it. Life on earth is not the real
thing. This is transition. This is not our home.' He defi-
nitely believed in life after death. He would mention
Jesus, although I never pushed him. 'You know there's
someone out there,' he would say. There was a gentle-
ness and tenderness in him I hadn't seen before. 'We're
here to help others,' he finally said to me. He was even
praying to God at the end." Summoning my courage, I
asked a question I couldn't believe I was asking, "Pastor,
do you think that at the end of his life, my father actually accepted Jesus Christ?" His surprising answer was
echoed by my father's nurse in an unexpected phone call
the next day.

She explained that she had gone to the bookstore on
Christmas Eve to buy my father a book for a birthday
present. Even to the end, my father had insisted on celebrating his birthday on Christmas even though he was
really born in early December. Since scrupulous records
were not kept at the time, no one knew precisely what
day my father had been born. Strangely Dad solved the
uncertainty by choosing Christmas as his birthday, say-

ing, "If Christmas was good enough for Jesus, it's good enough for me."

The nurse told me that she had given the book about Jesus to my father on Christmas Eve night. "He kept telling everyone about the book," she remarked. "He said, 'I believe. I've been saved. My daughter's been telling me for years. Now I understand the whole picture. If she hadn't gotten muscular dystrophy, she wouldn't be who she is today. Look how far she's come.'" By now, I was crying profusely as she continued, "There was no doubt in my mind that he was talking about the love of Jesus. There was no doubt in my mind." She paused to take a breath as her voice cracked. "There was a remarkable change in him in the last months. God was showing himself to him in so many little ways. He was able to see the tiny miracles. On a daily basis he could see them. The littlest things he was so in tune with. He said, 'This lady helped me with my scooter at the gate. Someone is up there looking out for me. Not all people stink.' It wasn't about him anymore or about self-pity. He was a very intelligent, loving man, you know, Beverly. It was God's timing—a beautiful moment when everything comes together." She paused again. "You know, Beverly, I normally don't do this, but do you mind if I have something of your father's? Every time I would give your father a bath, I would comment on the stone with the saying about faith that you gave him. It was sitting on the vanity, and I would always say, 'See, Mac, it's all about faith.'"

I had given that stone to my father years before and thought he had thrown it away. I was amazed that he hadn't. "Do you mind if I have it?" she asked hesitantly. "Of course you can," I mumbled through my tears. "I want you to have it." How fitting, I thought, to give her a stone in remembrance of my father that read, "Faith is daring the soul to go beyond what the eyes can see."

Sadly I was unable to visit my father in the days before his death, and he never told me that he had accepted Jesus. I still find myself wondering at times. I would have given anything to see his eyes opened to Jesus for the first time—and to be there when he died to witness the divine spark in his eyes before he closed them for the last time. Not that I needed to see evidence of the Divine to be convinced of God's reality. Ironically I had witnessed a divine spark in my mother's eyes when she died and came back to life, and I had found it hard to believe. This time I didn't have to see that spark in my father's eyes to know that God is not only the Source of life but also of new life.

I pray I was a thin place in my father's life. I hope with all my heart that Dad, a Jewish atheist, finally came to realize at the end of his life that he couldn't die without Jesus, just as his Jewish daughter, struck down by disease in the prime of her life, discovered that she couldn't live without him. What I do know for certain is that in the end, Dad and I were finally united in a spirit of reconciliation and forgiveness that could only have been brought about by the love of Jesus Christ.

How unimaginable it seems that Dad would actually accept Jesus in a most improbable epiphany. Yet when it comes to the Lord—and epiphanies—nothing is impossible. As Reverend Peter Gomes so eloquently preached during the season of Epiphany, "By the light of the glory of his countenance he shows us that we are the subject of his work, and that we are his work; and finally, in us will his glory be made manifest, for ultimately and truly and finally we are meant to be not simply witnesses to the epiphany of our Lord in the world: We *are* his epiphany."[5]

It is an awesome thought that because we are the Lord's epiphany on earth, we can be his vessels. For God not only shines his light upon us. He shines his light through us to others. However, many of us still yearn for Old Testament times, when we could witness the epiphany of our Lord as he manifested himself in dramatic and palpable ways. We find it difficult to bear witness to an invisible God, even one who dwells within us in the Holy Spirit. Nevertheless, we strive to "fix our eyes not on what is seen, but on what is unseen. For what is seen is temporary, but what is unseen is eternal" (2 Corinthians 4:18).

When it comes to the Lord—and epiphanies—nothing is impossible.

Fortunately, as Christians, we don't have to base our faith solely on the unseen. For when Jesus came to earth to die on a cross so that our sins would no longer come between us and God, he not only palpably revealed the promise of eternity to all who believed in him, he also visibly demonstrated that if we believe, we can meet him presently in a place of reconciliation, united in love—in a thin place.

On that blessed border between this world and the next, God is as close to us as we are to ourselves. We can feel his very breath on our face—the same breath he breathed into us when he gave us life.

As we reside in him, he resides in us. He is in our prayers and our meditations. He is in the good deeds we do and the suffering we must do. He is in our forgiveness and in our feeble attempts at selfless love. Through it all, he transforms us by shining his light upon us and through us to others, to redeem a fallen world and reclaim his creation.

For now, we see through a glass darkly (see 1 Corinthians 13:12, KJV). But it is only for a little while. In the blink of an eye, the veil will finally lift. The invisible will be made visible, and the unseen will finally be seen. On that glorious day, when we meet our Lord and Savior in heaven, we will not just feel his divine breath upon our face. We will literally behold him face-to-face.

> *We can feel God's very breath on our face—the same breath he breathed into us when he gave us life.*

In that breathtaking moment of death, will we rise as kindred spirits, rushing to embrace the risen Christ in joyful reunion? Or will we, even as Christians, be like strangers, reticent to approach our Lord because we barely knew him in life? Will we stand wide eyed, crying tears of gratitude because even in the darkness of our fallen world, we had times in life when we managed to find our way to that familiar Light? Or will we tearfully squint, our unaccustomed eyes struggling to let in the brilliance of an unfamiliar radiance that could have illuminated a lifetime of darkness, if only we had let it?

> *On that glorious day, when we meet our Lord and Savior in heaven, we will not just feel his divine breath upon our face. We will literally behold him face-to-face.*

The miracle of thin places is that they not only provide us with an opportunity to find illuminating moments this side of the other side. They also allow us to experience a living God of light, coming from the other side.

Such astonishing, divine encounters are amazing deposits of hope and promises of the glory to come. Even more, they are glorious moments of communion with a loving God who breaks through the veil daily because he longs to personally forge an everlasting relationship with us. In the process, not only are the ordinary moments of our lives transformed in extraordinary ways, but also so are we.

God reaches out to us in thin places, longing to touch us. We need only accept the grace of his loving embrace. The living Lord who breathed life into us miraculously draws so close, we can feel his breath—if we simply take notice.

We need only turn our face to the breeze—and believe.

In Gratitude

To Kathy Helmers, who by God's grace helped to make another seemingly impossible dream come true, thank you. You are a consummate mentor and incomparable ally. Even more, you are a cherished friend, touching my heart in ways few people ever have. You have enthusiastically escorted my physically challenged body up high mountains and compassionately comforted my struggling soul in deep valleys. Who else can turn my tears to laughter until I find myself laughing in tears? Who else can help me see so clearly what I have to give, when many others only see the little I seem to have? For all this and so much more, I am deeply and forever grateful.

To Doug Knox, Jan Long Harris, Lisa Jackson, Stephanie Voiland, Caleb Sjogren, Sharon Leavitt, and the rest of the Tyndale team, it has not only been a privilege and a pleasure working with you. It has also been a blessing.

To Patti Stadolnik, who changed my life with her giving heart, exuberant spirit, and keen mind, thank you. Your unwavering support, deep caring, and astute advice have meant more to me than you will ever know this side of heaven. It is a joy and a grace to call you my friend.

In Gratitude

To Pastor Dave Stewart, who encourages me with his humor, spiritual insights, and faith, thanks for everything. When I find myself searching for Jesus, I need look no further than the recesses of your loving heart.

To Kiersten Yanni, who allows me the privilege of loving and mentoring one of the most intelligent, compassionate, and brightest spirits I know, thank you. In this often frustrating fallen world, you embody not only the best of human nature but also the best of our future. It is a testament to your ability to so richly touch souls that you bring out the best in me even when I am far from my best. May the peace and love of Jesus be forever with you.

To Alice Crider, who braved many a deep spiritual conversation with this pilgrim, I am very grateful. You magnify and glorify the Spirit in a way that blesses all who are fortunate to know you. Thanks, my friend.

To Ed, who is not only a loving brother but also a loyal and trusted friend, thank you. Your unmatched intelligence, Jewish wit, and priceless perspectives on life never fail to spark my imagination, enriching and enlivening my days. Thanks for being so open to things you do not believe, for trying so hard to understand what you haven't experienced, and for supporting me in ventures you are not inclined to undertake—at least not yet. It takes an enormous heart and a generous spirit to so faithfully stand by me. The immeasurable love between us often remains unspoken, so let me say it here: I love you deeply and will love you forever.

Finally, to my mother, whom I love with a depth I could never adequately express, I am eternally grateful. You loved me first and kept loving me to the last. To my mother—my hero—I offer this tribute:

Love was all you knew.
Love was all you were.
And so I am certain,
That by God's grace,
Love is all there is.

Endnotes

Chapter 2: Discovering the Unseen

[1] Abraham Joshua Heschel, *God in Search of Man: A Philosophy of Judaism* (New York: Farrar, Straus and Giroux, 1983), 85.

[2] "Thin Places," http://www.thinplaces.net/ (accessed July 22, 2005).

[3] Harold S. Kushner, *To Life* (New York: Warner Books, 1993), 148.

[4] "Gandhian Institute," http://www.mkgandhi.org/momgandhi/chap10.htm (accessed July 22, 2005).

[5] Kushner, *To Life*, 151.

Chapter 3: Who Am I? Born of Divine Breath

[1] Kushner, *To Life*, 37.

[2] Abraham Cohen, *Everyman's Talmud: The Major Teachings of the Rabbinic Sages* (New York: E. P. Dutton, 1949), 73.

Chapter 4: When Am I? Eternity in Time

[1] Heschel, *God in Search of Man*, 418.

[2] Ibid.

[3] George Robinson, *Essential Judaism: A Complete Guide to Beliefs, Customs, and Rituals* (New York: Pocket Books, 2000), 222.

[4] Heschel, *God in Search of Man*, 359.

[5] Isaac Asimov, *Treasury of Humor* (New York: Houghton Mifflin Co., 1971), 240.

Chapter 5: Who Is God? The Unknowable Made Knowable

[1] Woody Allen, *Without Feathers, Getting Even, Side Effects* (New York: Quality Paperback Book Club, 1989), 6.

[2] Heschel, *God in Search of Man*, 85.

[3] Rabbi Joseph Telushkin, *Jewish Humor: What the Best Jewish Jokes Say About the Jews* (New York: William Morrow and Co., 1992), 147.

[4] Allen, *Without Feathers*, 25.

[5] Elie Wiesel, *Night* (New York: Bantam Books, 1960), 32.

[6] Elie Wiesel, in a speech given at the White House on April 12, 1999, entitled "The Perils of

Endnotes

Indifference," as quoted in The History Place, "Great Speeches Collection," copyright 1996–2005, http://www.historyplace.com/speeches/wiesel.htm (accessed July 22, 2005).

[7] Philip Yancey, *Where Is God When It Hurts?* (Grand Rapids: Zondervan, 1990), 157.

[8] Wiesel, *Night*, 62.

[9] Ibid., x.

[10] C. S. Lewis, *A Grief Observed* (San Francisco: HarperSanFrancisco, 1961), 34.

[11] Henry David Thoreau, *Walden* (Philadelphia: Courage Books, 1990), 12.

[12] Peter Kreeft, *Making Sense Out of Suffering* (Ann Arbor, Mich.: Servant Books, 1986), 12.

[13] C. S. Lewis, *The Problem of Pain* (New York: Macmillan Publishing Co., 1962), 108.

[14] Kreeft, *Making Sense*, 18.

[15] Heschel, *God in Search of Man*, 138.

[16] Kreeft, *Making Sense*, 164.

Chapter 6: Who Is Jesus? God Unveiled

[1] Kreeft, *Making Sense*, 133.

[2] Philip Yancey, *Disappointment with God* (Grand Rapids: Zondervan Publishing House, 1988), 225.

[3] Philip Yancey, *Where Is God When It Hurts?* (Grand Rapids: Zondervan Publishing House, 1990), 225.

[4] Kreeft, *Making Sense*, 130.

[5] Philip Yancey, *The Jesus I Never Knew* (Grand Rapids: Zondervan Publishing House, 1995), 159.

[6] Kushner, *To Life*, 158.

[7] Yancey, *Disappointment with God*, 183.

[8] Kreeft, *Making Sense*, 178.

[9] Peter J. Gomes, *The Good Book: Reading the Bible with Mind and Heart* (New York: HarperCollins, 1996), 228–29.

[10] Jane Johnson Struck, "Sweet Surrender," *Today's Christian Woman* (September/October 2004): 40.

Chapter 7: What Am I? Dust Falling, Spirit Rising

[1] Philip Yancey, *Reaching for the Invisible God* (Grand Rapids: Zondervan Publishing House, 2000), 116.

[2] Thomas Merton, *The Ascent to Truth* (San Diego: Harvest Books, 1979), 280.

[3] Allen P. Ross, *Creation and Blessing: A Guide to the Study and Exposition of Genesis* (Grand Rapids: Baker Books, 1998), 137.

[4] Yancey, *Reaching for the Invisible God*, 187.

[5] Richard J. Foster, *Streams of Living Water: Celebrating the Great Traditions of Christian Faith* (San Francisco: HarperSanFrancisco, 1998), 235.

[6] Yancey, *Reaching for the Invisible God*, 89.

[7] Thomas Merton, *New Seeds of Contemplation* (New York: New Directions Publishing Corp., 1972), 3.

Chapter 8: Why Am I? Made for Spiritual Embrace

[1] Morris N. Kertzer, *What Is a Jew?* (New York: Touchstone, 1996), 41.

[2] Richard Foster, *Celebration of Discipline: The Path to Spiritual Growth* (San Francisco: HarperSanFrancisco, 1998), 110.

[3] Ibid., 7.

[4] C. S. Lewis, *Letters to Malcolm: Chiefly on Prayer* (San Diego: Harcourt Brace, 1992), 58.

[5] Donald Spoto, *In Silence: Why We Pray* (New York: Viking Books, 2004), 129.

[6] P. T. Forsyth, *The Soul of Prayer* (Vancouver: Regent College Publishing, 2002), 12.

[7] Paula Huston, *The Holy Way: Practices for a Simple Life* (Chicago: Loyola Press, 2003), 311.

[8] A. W. Tozer, *The Pursuit of God* (Camp Hill, Penn.: Christian Publications, Inc., 1982), 45–46.

[9] Richard J. Foster, *Prayer: Finding the Heart's True Home* (New York: HarperCollins, 1992), 163.

[10] Brother Lawrence of the Resurrection, translated by John J. Delaney, *The Practice of the Presence of God* (New York: Doubleday, 1977), 55.

[11] Ibid., 49.

[12] Ibid., 51.

[13] Merton, *New Seeds*, 39.

[14] Foster, *Prayer*, 54–55.

[15] Simone Weil, *Gravity and Grace* (London and New York: Routledge Classics, 1999), 88–89.

Chapter 9: Where Am I? On the Border with Jesus

[1] Telushkin, *Jewish Humor*, 86.

[2] Ibid., 167.

[3] Anthony Bloom, *Beginning to Pray* (New York: Phoenix Press, 1970), 59–60.

[4] Howard E. Mumma, *Albert Camus and the Minister* (Brewster, Mass.: Paraclete Press, 2000), 28.

[5] Foster, *Prayer*, 248.

[6] Yancey, *Reaching for the Invisible God*, 84.

[7] Kreeft, *Making Sense*, 142.

Chapter 10: My Father and Me—and the Son?

[1] Corrie ten Boom, *Tramp for the Lord* (Grand Rapids: Fleming H. Revell Co., 1974), 55–57.

[2] Ibid.

[3] Peter J. Gomes, *Sermons: Biblical Wisdom for Daily Living* (New York: HarperCollins, 1998), 36.

[4] Foster, *Prayer*, 224.

[5] Gomes, *Sermons*, 36.

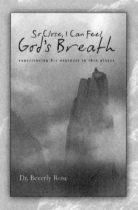

How an ordinary person
can learn to hear God speak

LISTENING *for*
GOD

*"Begin to recognize God's whispers
within your own heart."*
John C. Maxwell
Founder, The INJOY Group

Marilyn Hontz

Ｇod loves you deeply and longs to speak to you. The question is, are you listening?

With refreshing humility and openess, Marilyn Hontz explains how God taught her to reconize his voice and filled her with renewed purpose and an assurance of his unfailing love.

Listening for God will help you get beyond busyness and distractions and enable you to live out ordinary days with the extraordinary power that comes from hearing and listening to God's voice.

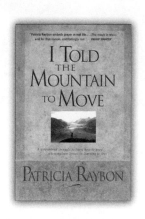

"The house was dark but also cold.
I opened my eyes in the dimness and sat up
straight, shivering. God was talking."

A discordant marriage. Conflicts with two strong-willed daughters. And underneath it all, a shameful personal secret. Believing God alone could move these mountains, Patricia Raybon set out to learn the real way to pray. Pray so things healed. Pray so things stopped. Pray so things started. Pray so things changed.

The result is an inspiring account of a journey that changed Patricia's world and transformed her heart—a journey full of lessons on prayer that will resonate with readers who long for deeper intimacy with an inscrutable, yet loving, God.